Learning Heroku Postgres

Efficiently design, implement, and manage a successful PostgreSQL database with Heroku

Patrick Espake

[PACKT] enterprise
PUBLISHING
professional expertise distilled

BIRMINGHAM - MUMBAI

Learning Heroku Postgres

First published: February 2015

Production reference: 1190215

Published by Packt Publishing Ltd.
Livery Place
35 Livery Street
Birmingham B3 2PB, UK.

ISBN 978-1-78217-345-8

www.packtpub.com

Credits

Author
Patrick Espake

Reviewers
Razvan Draghici
Andrea Mostosi
Peter Robinett
Karanraj Sankaranarayanan
Ariejan de Vroom

Commissioning Editor
Amarabha Bannerjee

Acquisition Editor
Nikhil Karkal

Content Development Editor
Pooja Nair

Technical Editor
Bharat Patil

Copy Editors
Karuna Narayanan
Laxmi Subramanian

Project Coordinator
Leena Purkait

Proofreaders
Stephen Copestake
Martin Diver
Paul Hindle

Indexer
Mariammal Chettiyar

Graphics
Disha Haria
Sheetal Aute

Production Coordinator
Alwin Roy

Cover Work
Alwin Roy

About the Author

Patrick Espake is passionate about technology, innovation, software development, and entrepreneurship. He has been professionally building and deploying web applications for over 10 years; with Heroku, it has been over 5 years, and he has worked on amazing projects for companies across the world. Currently, he is a cofounder of `http://coursify.me`. When Patrick isn't coding or writing, you will usually find him traveling to some wonderful place with his family.

I would like to thank my parents for their dedication and advice during my life, especially my mother, Elza, for not sparing effort and for her sacrifices to educate me and turn me into the person I am today. I would say that all your efforts were worthwhile and finishing this book together was a great achievement.

I also could never have finished this book without the support and encouraging words from my wife, Priscila. Through her infinite and pure love, she encouraged me and showed enormous patience during the several months that I've dedicated to this book. I would like to say that I am very grateful to be your husband.

I would also like to send a huge thank you to the Bard Kunenn family, who invited me numerous times for lunch during the weekends that I spent writing this book and provided me countless encouraging words for the creation of this book.

Finally, I would like to say thank you very much to my friend, Ana Carolina, for helping me in reviewing this book and for being so helpful with her suggestions for improvement.

About the Reviewers

Razvan Draghici is a full-stack software developer and scalability expert with over 7 years of experience in the field. In the past, he helped scale and develop high traffic applications for web properties, such as Sportsnet.ca, Bing Shopping Canada, and Canada Post Comparison Shopper. He is passionate about machine learning and data science, and while at Sportsnet he developed an NBA Playoffs winner prediction algorithm as part of a hackathon.

Razvan writes about software and technology at `http://sleekd.com`.

Andrea Mostosi is a technology enthusiast. An innovation lover since he was a child, he started his professional career in 2003 and worked on several projects, playing almost every role in the computer science environment. He is currently the CTO at The Fool, a company that tries to make sense of web and social data. During his free time, he likes to travel, run, cook, bike, and code.

> I would like to thank my geek friends: Simone M, Daniele V, Luca T, Luigi P, Michele N, Luca O, Luca B, Diego C, and Fabio B. They are the smartest people I know and comparing myself with them has always pushed me to be better.

Peter Robinett is a backend and mobile developer, focusing on Scala and iOS development. He is a frequent user of the Heroku platform and is a fan of its power and extensibility.

He is currently a developer at Lua Technologies. He also works under the name Bubble Foundry and blogs occasionally at `www.bubblefoundry.com`.

Ariejan de Vroom is a software engineer from Son en Breugel, The Netherlands. He's been working professionally with Ruby on Rails at Kabisa since 2007. When not writing code, Ariejan likes to read, play the piano and experiment with electronics.

Karanraj Sankaranarayanan is a certified Salesforce.com developer and works as a Salesforce consultant at HCL Technologies. He holds a bachelor's degree in engineering from Anna University with specialization in computer science. He has more than 4 years of experience in the Salesforce platform and IT industry. He is passionate about the Salesforce platform and is an active member of and contributor to the Salesforce developer community. He writes technical blogs at `http://clicksandcode.blogspot.in/`.

He won second place in the Salesforce Summer of Hacks event in Bangalore. He is also the organizer of the Chennai Salesforce Platform Developer Group based in Chennai, India. His Twitter handle is `@karanrajs`

www.PacktPub.com

Support files, eBooks, discount offers, and more

For support files and downloads related to your book, please visit www.PacktPub.com.

Did you know that Packt offers eBook versions of every book published, with PDF and ePub files available? You can upgrade to the eBook version at www.PacktPub.com and as a print book customer, you are entitled to a discount on the eBook copy. Get in touch with us at service@packtpub.com for more details.

At www.PacktPub.com, you can also read a collection of free technical articles, sign up for a range of free newsletters and receive exclusive discounts and offers on Packt books and eBooks.

https://www2.packtpub.com/books/subscription/packtlib

Do you need instant solutions to your IT questions? PacktLib is Packt's online digital book library. Here, you can search, access, and read Packt's entire library of books.

Why subscribe?

- Fully searchable across every book published by Packt
- Copy and paste, print, and bookmark content
- On demand and accessible via a web browser

Free access for Packt account holders

If you have an account with Packt at www.PacktPub.com, you can use this to access PacktLib today and view 9 entirely free books. Simply use your login credentials for immediate access.

Instant updates on new Packt books

Get notified! Find out when new books are published by following @PacktEnterprise on Twitter or the *Packt Enterprise* Facebook page.

Table of Contents

Preface

This book is a definitive guide on how to use PostgreSQL on Heroku. Learn how to work with backups, dataclips, rollback, followers, forks, extensions, PostGIS, data caching, tuning, log statements, and common errors.

Heroku Postgres allows you to manage your PostgreSQL databases in a simple, worry-free way and from anywhere. Through the offered features, you can easily scale your database and extend functionalities.

This book is suitable for all Heroku Postgres user levels and offers knowledge that will help you manage your database with tranquility. The book covers simple topics until we reach more complex issues such as data caching and tuning. Through this book, you will be able to work with all the functionalities provided by Heroku Postgres.

What this book covers

Chapter 1, Getting Started with Heroku Postgres, introduces the Heroku architecture and how to build applications using Heroku Postgres. It also describes the key concepts about Heroku.

Chapter 2, Heroku Toolbelt, describes the Heroku Toolbelt and all the necessary tools to get started using Heroku at the command-line.

Chapter 3, Postgres Add-on, covers how to configure your local development environment, how to use the add-on, how to create your database, and how to connect using different programming languages. It also introduces the concepts of monitoring and information logs.

Chapter 4, PG Backups, introduces how to generate backups, import/export databases, data security, continuous protection, and how to upgrade your database plan.

Chapter 5, Dataclips, describes how dataclips work and how to share them with your colleagues. It also provides knowledge about security and limitations.

Chapter 6, Rollback, Followers, and Forks, covers important concepts related to security, stability, and experiments in using PostgreSQL database on the Heroku platform. It discusses topics related to rollback, followers, and forks.

Chapter 7, Understanding Log Statements and Common Errors, introduces how to view logs, how to collect metrics, and how to understand the most common errors.

Chapter 8, Extensions, PostGIS, Full Text Search Dictionaries, Data Caching, and Tuning, describes a collection of advanced features: how to install the main extensions of the Postgres database, how to enable PostGIS for work with spatial data, how to make optimizations, the text search tools, and the data cache.

Appendix A, Keyword List, contains a set of keywords used in this book, along with their definitions to facilitate better understanding of the concepts.

Appendix B, Self-test Answers, contains the answers to questions in each chapter that help test the knowledge you acquired.

What you need for this book

The software needed for this book includes the Heroku Toolbelt (client) (`https://toolbelt.heroku.com`), your preferred IDE such as Sublime Text (`http://www.sublimetext.com`), PostgreSQL (`http://www.postgresql.org`), pgAdmin (`http://www.pgadmin.org`), the Google Chrome web browser, and a Terminal.

Who this book is for

Learning Heroku Postgres is suitable for developers and database administrators. Even if you are new to Heroku Postgres, you will be able to master both the basic functions and the advanced features of Heroku Postgres. Since Heroku Postgres maintains an incredibly user-friendly interface, no previous experience in computer coding or programming is required.

Conventions

In this book, you will find a number of styles of text that distinguish between different kinds of information. Here are some examples of these styles, and an explanation of their meaning.

Code words in text, database table names, folder names, filenames, file extensions, pathnames, dummy URLs, user input, and Twitter handles are shown as follows:

In the case of Ruby on Rails, these dependencies are found in `Gemfile` in Python `requirements.txt`, in Node.js `package.json`, and in Java `pom.xml`.

Any command-line input or output is written as follows:

```
$ heroku pg:info --app learning-heroku-postgres-app
```

New terms and **important words** are shown in bold. Words that you see on the screen, in menus or dialog boxes for example, appear in the text like this: "clicking the **Next** button moves you to the next screen".

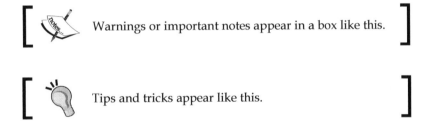

Warnings or important notes appear in a box like this.

Tips and tricks appear like this.

Reader feedback

Feedback from our readers is always welcome. Let us know what you think about this book—what you liked or may have disliked. Reader feedback is important for us to develop titles that you really get the most out of.

To send us general feedback, simply send an email to `feedback@packtpub.com`, and mention the book title via the subject of your message.

If there is a topic that you have expertise in and you are interested in either writing or contributing to a book, see our author guide on `www.packtpub.com/authors`.

Customer support

Now that you are the proud owner of a Packt book, we have a number of things to help you to get the most from your purchase.

Downloading the example code

You can download the example code files from your account at http://www.packtpub.com for all the Packt Publishing books you have purchased. If you purchased this book elsewhere, you can visit http://www.packtpub.com/support and register to have the files e-mailed directly to you.

Errata

Although we have taken every care to ensure the accuracy of our content, mistakes do happen. If you find a mistake in one of our books—maybe a mistake in the text or the code—we would be grateful if you would report this to us. By doing so, you can save other readers from frustration and help us improve subsequent versions of this book. If you find any errata, please report them by visiting http://www.packtpub.com/submit-errata, selecting your book, clicking on the **errata submission form** link, and entering the details of your errata. Once your errata are verified, your submission will be accepted and the errata will be uploaded on our website, or added to any list of existing errata, under the Errata section of that title. Any existing errata can be viewed by selecting your title from http://www.packtpub.com/support.

Piracy

Piracy of copyright material on the Internet is an ongoing problem across all media. At Packt, we take the protection of our copyright and licenses very seriously. If you come across any illegal copies of our works, in any form, on the Internet, please provide us with the location address or website name immediately so that we can pursue a remedy.

Please contact us at copyright@packtpub.com with a link to the suspected pirated material.

We appreciate your help in protecting our authors, and our ability to bring you valuable content.

Questions

You can contact us at questions@packtpub.com if you are having a problem with any aspect of the book, and we will do our best to address it.

1
Getting Started with Heroku Postgres

Heroku simplifies the infrastructure of web applications. With its architecture, it is possible to create robust, manageable, and scalable applications according to the needs of your business.

This book is focused on how Heroku works with PostgreSQL. It will cover pieces of architecture and how to build applications that benefit from Heroku Postgres. In this first chapter, you will learn about the key concepts of Heroku, how it works, what are the supported versions of PostgreSQL, how to choose the best plan according to your need, and how high availability works. The concepts covered in this chapter are fundamental to understanding the other chapters.

In this chapter, will cover the following topics:

- How does Heroku work?
- Postgres supported versions
- Choosing the right Heroku Postgres plan
- Production-tier technical characterization
- High availability

How does Heroku work?

Heroku is a multi-language cloud platform that enables you to deploy applications written in several programming languages such as Ruby, Java, Python, Clojure, Scala, and Node.js. The list of supported programming languages is always growing.

The main idea of Heroku is to take away the pain of managing and scaling servers, so you can focus on the development of your product and deliver more functionality to your client, where Heroku is responsible for the infrastructure.

You don't need knowledge of servers to build a robust application with millions of users around the world.

Heroku Dashboard and Heroku Toolbelt

Heroku has a dashboard where you can easily manage your application. Through this dashboard, you can manage your resources, dynos, workers, add-ons, metrics, activity log, access permissions, and settings. In this chapter, you will learn to better understand these items.

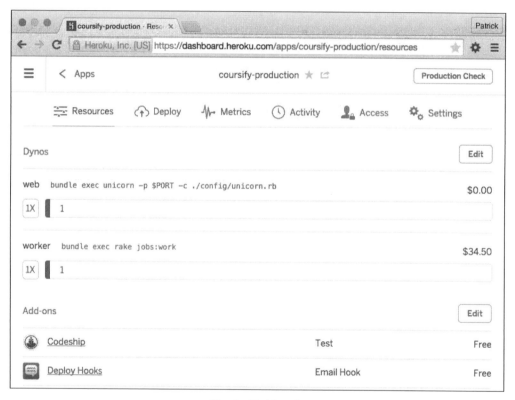

Heroku Dashboard

Heroku also provides a command-line client to manage your applications. This client is called Heroku Toolbelt and is available at `https://toolbelt.heroku.com`. It is available for Mac OS X, Windows, Debian/Ubuntu, or in standalone mode. Heroku Toolbelt is a set of tools for managing and displaying the information about your applications. Most developers prefer to use Heroku Toolbelt instead of Heroku Dashboard because of the command-line facilities, in addition to offering a broader set of information. In the following chapter, you will understand how it works.

Heroku Toolbelt

Deploying your applications

The first item you need to understand is how the deploy process happens. An application is a collection of code with its associated dependencies. In the case of Ruby on Rails, these dependencies are found in `Gemfile` in Python `requirements.txt`, in Node.js `package.json`, and in Java `pom.xml`. This gives further information on how Heroku should work with your code.

If you use Ruby, Node.js, Python, or Java, Heroku can easily identify how to make your code executable, through the conventions that these languages adopt. For example, in the case of Ruby on Rails, Heroku knows it needs to run the Rails server to run your application.

If Heroku cannot run your application, you need to show how to do it. You must do so through the creation of a `Procfile` in your project, which contains instructions on how to run your application, as follows:

```
web: java -jar lib/my_app.jar $PORT
```

Downloading the example code

You can download the example code files from your account at `http://www.packtpub.com` for all the Packt Publishing books you have purchased. If you purchased this book elsewhere, you can visit `http://www.packtpub.com/support` and register to have the files e-mailed directly to you.

Heroku has adopted a very simple way to send your code to deploy. Each application built on Heroku has a Git repository, you should do a `git push heroku master` to start the deploy process. In the next chapter, you will deploy your first application and understand it better.

Heroku handles your code and dependencies by generating an optimized slug of your application. This slug is placed in each dyno that you have and each slug contains a compressed copy of your application. The slug is created by the slug compiler and its core is a collection of scripts called a buildpack. For each language supported by Heroku, there is one buildpack available. You can find more information about each of them in their repositories on GitHub:

- **Clojure**: `https://github.com/heroku/heroku-buildpack-clojure`
- **Gradle**: `https://github.com/heroku/heroku-buildpack-gradle`
- **Grails**: `https://github.com/heroku/heroku-buildpack-grails`
- **Java**: `https://github.com/heroku/heroku-buildpack-java`
- **Node.js**: `https://github.com/heroku/heroku-buildpack-nodejs`
- **PHP**: `https://github.com/heroku/heroku-buildpack-php`
- **Play**: `https://github.com/heroku/heroku-buildpack-play`
- **Python**: `https://github.com/heroku/heroku-buildpack-python`
- **Ruby**: `https://github.com/heroku/heroku-buildpack-ruby`
- **Scala**: `https://github.com/heroku/heroku-buildpack-scala`

The dyno manager is responsible for managing each dyno with your application slug.

Heroku architecture

Heroku's architecture is very robust and equipped to work with small applications such as blogs, personal websites, and large applications with a lot of users, such as Ello and Toyota.

This architecture serves the entire operation flow of its application, providing the mechanism to deploy your code until the management and scalability of your application.

The following diagram shows this architecture:

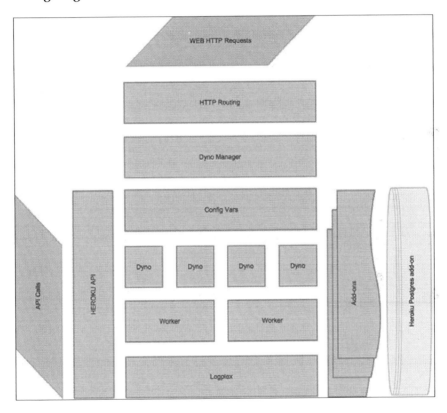

HTTP routing

The Heroku platform receives HTTP requests coming from the entry point herokuapp.com or by your custom domain, and forwards these requests to the load balancer, then to the routing mesh that distributes it for each dyno. The routing mesh is a personalized solution developed in Erlang based on MochiWeb (https://github.com/mochi/mochiweb). Each dyno has its own queue of requests to be processed. When a dyno is available, it picks up a request from its queue and the application inside the dyno processes it.

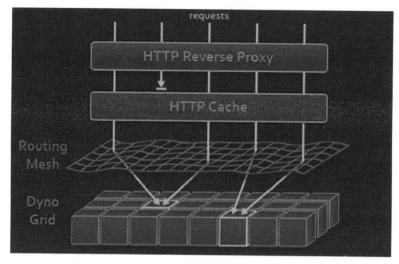

Heroku HTTP routing

Dyno Manager

The Dyno Manager is responsible for maintaining the dynos running. When some dyno presents a problem, it is automatically replaced by a new dyno and the application information is loaded through the slug generated during the deploy. Because of the Dyno Manager, you do not need to make any changes to the operating system or other internal settings. Everything is done in an automated way.

Config vars

The traditional approach is setting the configuration variables in the source code of your application; this approach is not useful, especially when you have many environments such as production, development, and test. The safer approach is creating environment variables. Heroku works with environment variables called config vars.

Config vars are necessary to run your application. Some of these variables are provided by Heroku and others are provided by add-ons that you have installed. You can also add your own config vars. For example, for Postgres add-on the config vars are provided credentials to access the database. All the provided dynos have the same set of config vars. These variables are copied automatically when you create a new dyno.

Understanding the Dynos

A dyno is a single virtualization in a Unix container. This container contains the slug of your application created during the deploy and you can add more dynos at anytime for scaling your application. The dyno does not persist changes in the filesystem and does not contain a database. To save files, you need to use a shared service such as Amazon AWS S3 (Simple Storage Service), and use the data store's add-ons such as Heroku Postgres, ClearDB MySQL Database, MongoLab (MongoDB), Redis Cloud, GrapheneDB, or others to share a database data between your dynos. You can see all the available data stores' add-ons at `https://addons.heroku.com/#data-stores`.

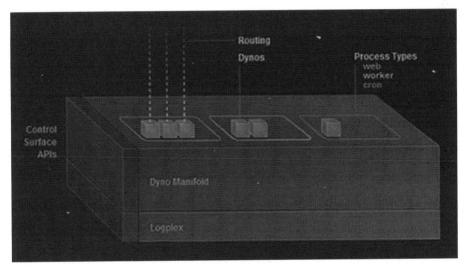

Heroku Dynos

Workers

Workers are responsible for running background jobs in your applications hosted on Heroku. This is a key feature for building really scalable web applications. Through the workers, your applications can resize images, perform data upload to other servers, fetch API data, send e-mail, and perform many other tasks in the background. Your web requests always return immediately improving the user experience. On Heroku, the workers are scalable, so you can increase or decrease the quantity at anytime.

Add-ons

Heroku has a marketplace of add-ons. The idea of these add-ons is to provide integration with third-party services simply and seamlessly into your applications hosted on Heroku. Currently, there is a wide variety of add-ons that are divided in categories: Data Stores, Mobile, Search, Logging, e-mail, SMS, Workers and Queueing, Analytics, Caching, Monitoring, Media, Utilities, and Payments. Add-ons include Heroku Postgres, PG Backups, MemCachier, AirBrake, New Relic APM, Logentries, Deploy Hooks, Heroku Scheduler, Zerigo DNS, SSL, Websolr, SendGrid, Mandrill by MailChimp, and Codeship. You can meet these add-ons at `https://addons.heroku.com/`.

PostgreSQL is provided on Heroku via an add-on called Heroku Postgres. This add-on has a number of plans that vary in their features such as cache size, storage limit, limit of simultaneous connections, and the ability to work with forks and followers. In the *Choosing the right Heroku Postgres plan* section, you will understand more about these differences.

Logplex

Logplex is a distributed log collector, able to merge and redistribute multiple input streams to individual subscribers. Logs are collected from your app and other components of the Heroku platform. You can query this information through the Heroko Toolbelt or using the public API Logplex. These logs are collected from all the dynos and components that you have on Heroku.

Heroku API

The Heroku platform API allows you to create automated tasks, such as creating applications, collecting information from applications, managing add-ons, or performing other tasks programmatically, which previously could only be done through the Heroku dashboard. For example, Heroku Toolbelt uses Heroku API to perform its tasks.

Postgres supported versions

PostgreSQL is a relational database, open source, and very powerful. It has over 20 years of development and has a proved and reliable architecture. It is commonly adopted in many applications because of the following advantages:

- An open-source SQL standard compliant RDBMS
- Strong community
- Strong third-party support
- Extensible
- Objective

PostgreSQL is provided on Heroku via an add-on. This add-on has a free initial plan, only for small applications such as websites or blogs and then is available at a given series of paid plans, according to your need.

Each year a new version of PostgreSQL is released and Heroku adopts the newest version as standard in a very short time. Heroku keeps the current version and the last three versions. The versions currently available are:

- 9.4 (beta)
- 9.3 (default)
- 9.2
- 9.1
- 9.0 (deprecated, support ended December 3, 2014)

This means that every three years you need to upgrade the version of PostgreSQL used in your application because a new version of PostgreSQL is available and the last one is deprecated.

Choosing the right Heroku Postgres plan

Heroku offers three lines of plans with some differences in characteristics, these changes were made to suit small applications to applications that have a large volume of data or need transactional control.

Choosing the best plan will depend on the needs of your application. At any time, you can upgrade your database plan and optimize your application with a very short period of downtime. You will see more information about this in *Chapter 6, Rollback, Followers, and Forks*.

The main variations between the plans are expected downtime supported:

- Hobby tier tolerates 4 hours of downtime and is used for small and simple applications.

- Standard tier tolerates 1 hour of downtime and is used for production applications.

- Premium tier tolerates 15 minutes of downtime and is used for production applications where uptime is important.

The uptime expectations are measured based on a 30-day month.

The following table shows the main differences between the plans offered by Heroku and their respective prices:

Plan	Connection Limit	Row Limit	RAM	Storage	Price
Hobby Dev	20	10,000	0 Bytes	No	Free
Hobby Basic	20	10,000,000	0 Bytes	No	$9/mo
Standard 0	120	Unlimited	1 GB	64 GB	$50/mo
Premium 0	120	Unlimited	1 GB	64 GB	$200/mo
Standard 2	400	Unlimited	3.5 GB	256 GB	$200/mo
Premium 2	400	Unlimited	3.5 GB	256 GB	$350/mo
Standard 4	500	Unlimited	15 GB	512 GB	$750/mo
Premium 4	500	Unlimited	15 GB	512 GB	$1200/mo
Standard 5	500	Unlimited	30 GB	1 TB	$1400/mo
Standard 6	500	Unlimited	60 GB	1 TB	$2000/mo
Premium 5	500	Unlimited	30 GB	1 TB	$2500/mo
Premium 6	500	Unlimited	60 GB	1 TB	$3500/mo
Standard 7	500	Unlimited	120 GB	1 TB	$3500/mo
Premium 7	500	Unlimited	120 GB	1 TB	$6000/mo

Shared features

All the plans share the following features:

- Data clips to share data and queries with others people securely
- SSL protection to access psql/libpq
- Postgres extensions
- Web UI interface to manage the database

- Unmodified versions of Postgres
- Database service fully managed for automatic health checks
- Write-ahead log (WAL) that ensures minimal data loss in case of catastrophic failure, storing every minute

Production-tier technical characterization

The Standard, Premium, and Enterprise plans are offered for production applications that require certain operating characteristics based on multitenancy architectures, CPU, RAM, and IO. These characteristics can be more easily understood with the help of the following table:

Plan	vCPU	RAM	Disk Size	Connection Limit	PIOPs	Multitenant
Standard 0						
Premium 0	2	1 GB	64 GB	120	200	Yes
Standard 2						
Premium 2	2	3.5 GB	256 GB	400	200	Yes
Standard 4						
Premium 4	2	15 GB	512 GB	500	1000	No
Standard 5						
Premium 5	4	30 GB	1 TB	500	2000	No
Standard 6						
Premium 6	8	60 GB	1 TB	500	3000	No
Standard 7						
Premium 7						
Enterprise 7	16	120 GB	1 TB	500	4000	No
Enterprise 8	32	240 GB	1 TB	500	4000	No

All plans run a 64-bit architecture, which ensures the best performance for the internal operations of Postgres. Heroku Postgres runs on a virtual infrastructure provided by Amazon AWS EC2.

The vCPU is the number of virtual processors in the instance and RAM is the amount of memory used to data cache. The PIOPs are a measure of how many IO disk operations can be performed per second.

For applications that require a lot of writes, IO can be a critical point. The data sets should fit in RAM, which ensures high performance with lower values of IOPs (Input/Output operations per second).

Finally, multitenancy refers to the principle of software architecture where a software instance is a server serving multiple client organizations (tenants).

High availability

The plans of the Premium and Enterprise tier comes with the High Availability feature. This feature involves a cluster database and a management system to increase availability in case of failure.

When the database fails, it is automatically replaced by another. To determine that a failure occurred, Heroku starts a series of checks. This process can take up to 2 minutes. Because of the continuous protection mechanism, Heroku minimizes data loss, usually to 160 MB or 10 minutes, whichever is less.

When the recovery process finishes, new access credentials are generated and the database URL is changed. Finally the Heroku application is restarted with the new access data to the database.

Self-test Questions

Answer true or false:

1. Is Heroku a multi-language platform?
2. Using Heroku, does the developer have many concerns about infrastructure?
3. Is Heroku Toolbelt the most powerful way to manage your apps on Heroku?
4. Is it possible to deploy applications on Heroku via FTP?
5. Is dyno a virtualization of a Unix container?
6. Does Heroku always support the latest 10 versions of PostgreSQL?
7. Do the plans of the Premium tier tolerate 30 minutes of downtime?
8. Do all plans of Heroku run a 64-bit architecture?
9. Do only Standard plans have the capability of High Availability?
10. When a new database is built upon failure access, are the credentials changed?

Summary

In this chapter, you have learned how Heroku works, how to transform your application into a slug with dependencies that can be distributed across multiple dynos, making your application scalable. You have also learned that by default Heroku supports the current version of PostgreSQL and the last three versions, and every three years you need to upgrade the version used in your application.

You have also learned about the structure of the Heroku plans and your characteristics, where the Hobby plans are more oriented for blogs or personal websites, while the Standard, Premium, and Enterprise plans are ideal for production applications. You understood that the downtime of each plan must be taken into consideration to choose the plan that is best for your business.

You also got knowledge about the characterization of the Standard, Premium, and Enterprise plans and that there are variations of plans based on the usage of vCPU, RAM, and IO.

Finally, you learned the High Availability feature that manages and monitors the application and database in case of a failure. When a new database is created, the credentials are changed.

In the next chapter, you will learn about the Heroku Toolbelt and all tools you need to get started with using Heroku at the command line.

2
Heroku Toolbelt

Heroku Toolbelt is a powerful command-line tool. With it you can manage your apps and perform many tasks such as create applications, configure add-ons, take backups, add new dynos, and so on. The vast majority of activities require that Heroku Toolbelt be installed.

In this chapter, we will cover the following topics:

- Signing up
- Installing the Heroku Toolbelt
- Logging in to Heroku
- Deploying an application

Signing up

To start using Heroku, first you need to create a user account. For this, visit the Heroku website (`https://www.heroku.com`), click on **Sign up**, and follow the registration instructions provided by Heroku.

The following screenshot displays the Sign up page of Heroku:

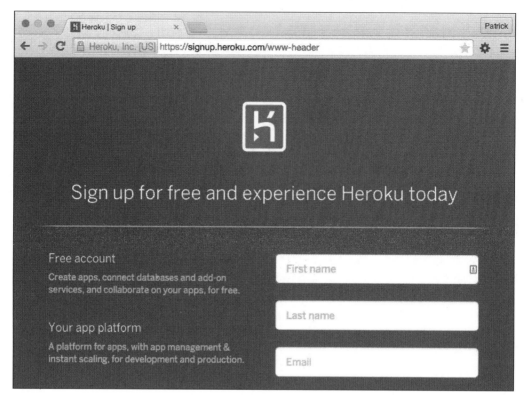

Heroku Signup

Installing the Heroku Toolbelt

Heroku Toolbelt is available for download at `https://toolbelt.heroku.com` for Mac OS X, Windows, Debian/Ubuntu, and standalone operating systems. Choose your operating system, download, and install it.

For Mac OS X, Windows, and Debian/Ubuntu, the following software applications are automatically installed if you don't have them installed on your computer:

- **Heroku client**: This is the client tool to create and manage your Heroku applications
- **Foreman**: This is the tool used to run your applications locally
- **Git**: This is the distributed revision control system used to manage and deploy your Heroku applications

If you choose the standalone version, only the Heroku client is installed and you must install Foreman and Git manually. You can find more information about the installation for your operating system at `https://github.com/ddollar/foreman` and `http://git-scm.com`.

Logging in to Heroku

For using the Heroku Toolbelt, you need to log in via the command line. After this, you can start working with Heroku.

For log in, you must provide the e-mail and password used when you created your user account. If you are using Mac OS X or any Linux distribution, you will have to open a Terminal window. If you are using Windows, you must open the Command Prompt and type the following command to login:

```
$ heroku login
Enter your Heroku credentials.
Email: your-username@your-company.com
Password (typing will be hidden):
Authentication successful.
```

Heroku also needs your SSH public key as it identifies which developer is making changes in the applications. It's very simple to send your public key:

```
$ heroku keys:add
Found existing public key: /Users/patrickespake/.ssh/id_rsa.pub
Uploading SSH public key /Users/patrickespake/.ssh/id_rsa.pub... done
```

Now you're able to use all the commands that the Heroku client provides.

Deploying an application

Heroku allows you to deploy apps in Ruby, Python, Node.js, PHP, Java, Scala, and Clojure, as well as web frameworks that each language implements.

> The list of support languages are always growing up and you can find all of them at `https://devcenter.heroku.com/categories/language-support`.

A Heroku application consists of its source code, the dependencies mapping, and `Procfile`; the last one is important for Heroku because it describes the command to be executed to start your application and other processes. However, usually Heroku can discover the necessary processes for most languages and applications automatically, you don't even need to worry about that. If you need more advanced features, you'll find it at `https://devcenter.heroku.com/articles/procfile`.

How to deploy a simple application in Ruby on Rails in order to display the concepts to deploy Heroku applications is shown in the upcoming topics. The process is very similar to other programming languages and you can find more information at `https://devcenter.heroku.com/articles/quickstart#step-4-deploy-an-application`.

The sample application source code

You will deploy a sample application prepared with Ruby on Rails. This application is very simple; it just shows a welcome page and you can find it at `https://github.com/patrickespake/ruby-getting-started`. It's a helpful method for you to understand the main concepts about the deploy process on Heroku.

 You don't need the Ruby on Rails environment on your local computer for following this example, the sample application has everything you need to deploy your first application on Heroku.

First you need to copy the sample application source code. This basically consists of executing the `git clone` command in your terminal if you have a user account on GitHub:

```
git clone git@github.com:patrickespake/ruby-getting-started.git
cd ruby-getting-started
```

The other alternative is downloading the source code from `https://github.com/patrickespake/ruby-getting-started/archive/master.zip`.

The dependencies file

Heroku recognizes a Ruby application through the existence of a dependency file named `Gemfile`. Take a look at this file; you will see the following dependencies for the sample application:

```
source 'https://rubygems.org'

# Bundle edge Rails instead: gem 'rails', github: 'rails/rails'
```

```
gem 'rails', '4.1.8'
# Use postgresql as the database for Active Record
gem 'pg'
# Run Rails the 12factor way
gem 'rails_12factor', group: :production
# Use SCSS for stylesheets
gem 'sass-rails', '~> 4.0.3'
# Use Uglifier as compressor for JavaScript assets
gem 'uglifier', '>= 1.3.0'
# Use CoffeeScript for .js.coffee assets and views
gem 'coffee-rails', '~> 4.0.0'
# Use jquery as the JavaScript library
gem 'jquery-rails'
# Turbolinks makes following links in your web application faster.
  Read more: https://github.com/rails/turbolinks
gem 'turbolinks'
# Build JSON APIs with ease. Read more: https://github.com/rails/jbuilder
gem 'jbuilder', '~> 2.0'
# bundle exec rake doc:rails generates the API under doc/api.
gem 'sdoc', '~> 0.4.0',        group: :doc
# Spring speeds up development by keeping your application running in
  the background. Read more: https://github.com/rails/spring
gem 'spring',         group: :development
# Use unicorn as the app server
gem 'unicorn'
```

Deploying the sample application

First you will create a new Heroku application. Before executing the following command, check that you are inside the ruby-getting-started directory:

```
$ heroku create
Creating mighty-atoll-7219... done, stack is cedar-14
https://mighty-atoll-7219.herokuapp.com/ | https://git.heroku.com/mighty-atoll-7219.git
Git remote heroku added
```

A new application was created with the name `mighty-atoll-7219` and provided at `https://mighty-atoll-7219.herokuapp.com`. This URL will start working only after the first deploy. A Git repository was also created. This repository is available at `https://git.heroku.com/mighty-atoll-7219.git` and you can also add it using the `git [some action] heroku` command.

Finally, for starting the deploy, just type the command:

```
$ git push heroku master
Counting objects: 168, done.
Delta compression using up to 4 threads.
Compressing objects: 100% (110/110), done.
Writing objects: 100% (168/168), 30.31 KiB | 0 bytes/s, done.
Total 168 (delta 46), reused 164 (delta 43)
Compressing source files... done.
Building source:


-----> Ruby app detected
-----> Compiling Ruby/Rails
-----> Using Ruby version: ruby-2.0.0
-----> Installing dependencies using 1.7.12
       Running: bundle install --without development:test --path
         vendor/bundle --binstubs vendor/bundle/bin -j4 --deployment
       Fetching gem metadata from https://rubygems.org/...........
       Installing rake 10.4.0
       Installing i18n 0.6.11
       ...
-----> Preparing app for Rails asset pipeline
       Running: rake assets:precompile
       ...


-----> Discovering process types
       Procfile declares types -> web
       Default types for Ruby  -> console, rake, worker


-----> Compressing... done, 27.0MB
-----> Launching... done, v6
       https://mighty-atoll-7219.herokuapp.com/ deployed to Heroku
```

```
Verifying deploy... done.
To https://git.heroku.com/mighty-atoll-7219.git
...
```

> You don't need to worry about costs at this moment. When you create a new application, just one dyno is used and it's free.

Visiting the sample application

At this point, you can see the sample application. Type the following command:

```
$ heroku open
```

As the preceding command is fired you get the following output:

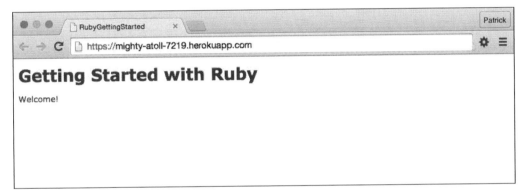

Deploying the Ruby app

Self-test questions

Answer true or false:

1. When installing Heroku Toolbelt, is standalone Git also provided?
2. Does Heroku also support web frameworks of the languages Ruby, Java, Python, Clojure, Scala, and Node.js?
3. Is Foreman a tool provided to run applications locally?
4. To deploy a Heroku app, do we only require the source code and dependencies file?
5. Does Heroku provide a web address to see the applications?

Summary

You learned the basics to get started with Heroku. You created your user account, learned how to install Heroku Toolbelt, how to create a Heroku application, and how to deploy your applications.

You also understood that Heroku needs three components to deploy: the source code, the dependencies file, and Procfile which describes what command should be executed to start your application.

So, the concepts learned in this chapter are fundamental to the rest of this book.

In the next chapter, you will learn about Postgres add-ons. You will create your first database and learn how to connect with different programming languages. In addition, you will learn about database permissions and monitoring.

3
Postgres Add-on

In this chapter, you will learn about the Postgres add-on, how to configure your local development environment, how to use the add-on, how to create your database, and how to connect using different programming languages. In addition, you will learn about connection permissions, how to connect in the database, and how to use databases that are not hosted on Heroku. You will also learn the first concepts of monitoring, information logs, and how to remove the add-on.

In this chapter, we will cover the following topics:

- Local setup
- Creating a new app
- Adding the add-on and creating the first database
- The Heroku Postgres web interface
- Using the Heroku client with Postgres
- Connecting with Java
- Connecting with Ruby
- Connecting with Python
- Connecting with Node.js
- Connection permissions
- External connections
- Connecting to databases from outside Heroku
- Monitoring and logging
- Removing the add-on

Local setup

You need to install PostgreSQL on your computer; this installation is recommended because some commands of the Postgres add-on require PostgreSQL to be installed. Besides that, it's a good idea for your development database to be similar to your production database; this avoids problems between these environments.

Next, you will learn how to set up PostgreSQL on Mac OS X, Windows, and Linux. In addition to pgAdmin, this is the most popular and rich feature in PostgreSQL's administration and development platform.

The versions recommended for installation are PostgreSQL 9.4.0 and pgAdmin 1.20.0, or the latest available versions.

Setting up PostgreSQL on Mac OS X

The **Postgres.app** application is the simplest way to get started with PostgreSQL on Mac OS X, it contains many features in a single installation package:

- PostgreSQL 9.4.0
- PostGIS 2.1.4
- Procedural languages: PL/pgSQL, PL/Perl, PL/Python, and PLV8 (JavaScript)
- Popular extensions such as hstore, uuid-ossp, and others
- Many command-line tools for managing PostgreSQL and convenient tools for GIS

The following screenshot displays the postgresapp website:

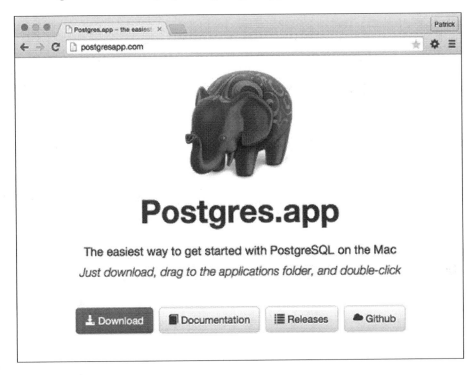

For installation, visit the address `http://postgresapp.com/`, carry out the appropriate download, drag it to the applications directory, and then double-click to open.

The other alternatives for installing PostgreSQL are to use the default graphic installer, Fink, MacPorts, or Homebrew. All of them are available at `http://www.postgresql.org/download/macosx`.

To install pgAdmin, you should visit `http://www.pgadmin.org/download/macosx.php`, download the latest available version, and follow the installer instructions.

Setting up PostgreSQL on Windows

PostgreSQL on Windows is provided using a graphical installer that includes the PostgreSQL server, pgAdmin, and the package manager that is used to download and install additional applications and drivers for PostgreSQL.

To install PostgreSQL, visit http://www.postgresql.org/download/windows, click on the download link, and select the the appropriate Windows version: 32 bit or 64 bit. Follow the instructions provided by the installer.

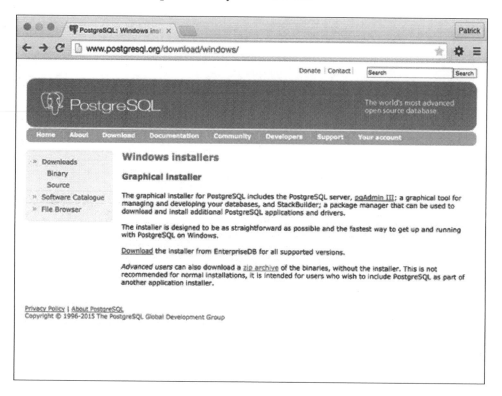

After installing PostgreSQL on Windows, you need to set the PATH environment variable so that the psql, pg_dump and pg_restore commands can work through the Command Prompt. Perform the following steps:

1. Open **My Computer**.

2. Right-click on **My Computer** and select **Properties**.

3. Click on **Advanced System Settings**.

4. Click on the **Environment Variables** button.

5. From the **System variables** box, select the **Path** variable.

6. Click on **Edit**.

7. At the end of the line, add the bin directory of PostgreSQL: c:\Program Files\PostgreSQL\9.4\bin;c:\Program Files\PostgreSQL\9.4\lib.

8. Click on the **OK** button to save.

The directory follows the pattern `c:\Program Files\PostgreSQL\VERSION\...`, check your PostgreSQL version.

Setting up PostgreSQL on Linux

The great majority of Linux distributions already have PostgreSQL in their package manager. You can search the appropriate package for your distribution and install it. If your distribution is Debian or Ubuntu, you can install it with the following command:

```
$ sudo apt-get install postgresql
```

If your Linux distribution is Fedora, Red Hat, CentOS, Scientific Linux, or Oracle Enterprise Linux, you can use the YUM package manager to install PostgreSQL:

```
$ sudo yum install postgresql94-server
$ sudo service postgresql-9.4 initdb
$ sudo chkconfig postgresql-9.4 on
$ sudo service postgresql-9.4 start
```

If your Linux distribution doesn't have PostgreSQL in your package manager, you can install it using the Linux installer. Just visit the website `http://www.postgresql.org/download/linux`, choose the appropriate installer, 32-bit or 64-bits, and follow the install instructions.

You can install `pgAdmin` through the package manager of your Linux distribution; for Debian or Ubuntu you can use the following command:

```
$ sudo apt-get install pgadmin3
```

For Linux distributions that use the YUM package manager, you can install through the following command:

```
$ sudo yum install pgadmin3
```

If your Linux distribution doesn't have pgAdmin in its package manager, you can download and install it following the instructions provided at `http://www.pgadmin.org/download/`.

Creating a local database

For the examples in this chapter, you will need to have a local database created. You will create a new database called `my_local_database` through pgAdmin.

To create the new database, perform the following steps:

1. Open pgAdmin.
2. Connect to the database server through the access credentials that you chose in the installation process.
3. Click on the **Databases** item in the tree view.
4. Click on the menu **Edit -> New Object -> New database**.
5. Type the name `my_local_database` for the database.
6. Click on the **OK** button to save.

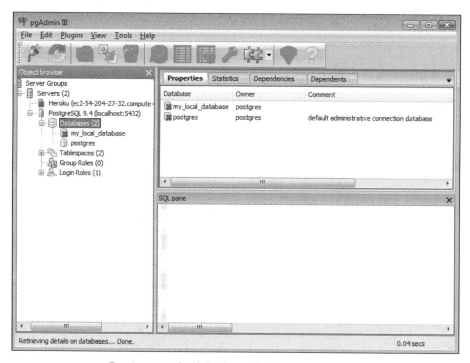

Creating a new local database called my_local_database

Creating a new app

Many features in Heroku can be implemented in two different ways; the first is via the Heroku client, which is installed through the Heroku Toolbelt, and the other is through the web Heroku dashboard.

In this section, you will learn how to use both of them.

Via the Heroku dashboard

Access the website `https://dashboard.heroku.com` and login. After that, click on the plus sign at the top of the dashboard to create a new app and the following screen will be shown:

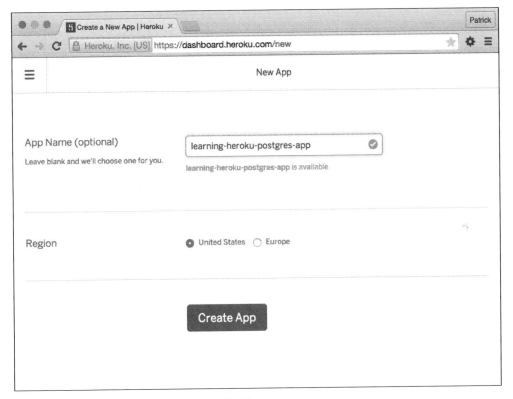

Creating an app

In this step, you should provide the name of your application. In the preceding example, it's **learning-heroku-postgres-app**. You can choose a name you prefer. Select which region you want to host it on; two options are available: **United States** or **Europe**.

Heroku doesn't allow duplicated names for applications; each application name supplied is global and, after it has been used once, it will not be available for another person. It can happen that you choose a name that is already being used. In this case, you should choose another name.

Choose the best option for you, it is usually recommended you select the region that is closest to you to decrease server response time. Click on the **Create App** button.

Then Heroku will provide some information to perform the first deploy of your application. The website URL and Git repository are created using the following addresses: `http://learning-heroku-postgres-app.herokuapp.com` and `git@heroku.com/learning-heroku-postgres-app.git`.

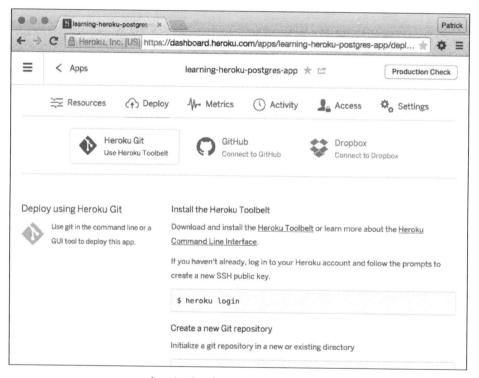

learning-heroku-postgres-app created

Next you will create a directory in your computer and link it with Heroku to perform future deployments of your source code. Open your terminal and type the following commands:

```
$ mkdir your-app-name
$ cd your-app-name
```

```
$ git init
$ heroku git:remote -a your-app-name
Git remote heroku added
```

Finally, you are able to deploy your source code at any time through these commands:

```
$ git add .
$ git commit -am "My updates"
$ git push heroku master
```

Via the Heroku client

Creating a new application via the Heroku client is very simple. The first step is to create the application directory on your computer. For that, open the Terminal and type the following commands:

```
$ mkdir your-app-name
$ cd your-app-name
$ git init
```

After that you need to create a new Heroku application through the command:

```
$ heroku apps:create your-app-name
Creating your-app-name... done, stack is cedar-14
https://your-app-name.herokuapp.com/ | HYPERLINK "https://git.heroku.
com/your-app-name.git" https://git.heroku.com/your-app-name.git
Git remote heroku added
```

Finally, you are able to deploy your source code at any time through these commands:

```
$ git add .
$ git commit -am "My updates"
$ git push heroku master
```

 Another very common case is when you already have a Git repository on your computer with the application's source code and you want to deploy it on Heroku. In this case, you must run the heroku apps:create your-app-name command inside the application directory and the link with Heroku will be created.

Adding the add-on and creating the first database

Heroku Postgres is accessible via any programming language by the connection driver of PostgreSQL; this includes all languages and frameworks supported by Heroku, such as Java, Ruby, Python, Scala, Play, Node.js, and Clojure.

Adding the Heroku Postgres add-on

You can add the Heroku Postgres add-on in two different ways: via the Heroku add-ons gallery or the Heroku client.

Via the Heroku add-ons gallery

Heroku offers a gallery of add-ons for your applications, this gallery is available at `https://addons.heroku.com/`.

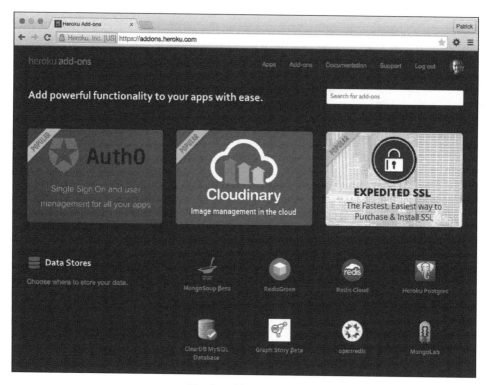

Heroku add-ons gallery

In the **Data Stores** area, you can find the **Heroku Postgres** add-on or you can find it at `https://addons.heroku.com/heroku-postgresql`.

 Before installing the Heroku Postgres add-on, you must log in to Heroku.

As shown in the first chapter, this add-on has many plans that change according to the functionality of the cache size, storage limit, the simultaneous connection limit, high availability, and the ability to work with forks and followers. You can choose the best plan for yourself, but if you prefer jumping straight in it's advisable to choose the `Hobby Dev` plan, which is free and ideal for small data sets with a maximum of 10,000 lines.

At the bottom of the website, choose the application and click on the **Add Hobby Dev for Free** button so that you can add the **Heroku Postgres** add-on in your application.

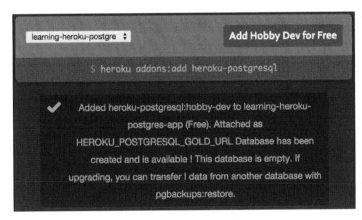

Add Heroku Postgres add-on

Via the Heroku client

Adding the Heroku Postgres add-on via the Heroku client is simple and fast.

 You can use the `--app` flag to always specify which application you are working with. This flag is optional; if you are inside the application directory in your computer, you don't need to use it.

Open a terminal in your computer and type the following command:

```
$ heroku addons:add heroku-postgresql:hobby-dev --app your-app-name
Adding heroku-postgresql:hobby-dev on your-app-name... done, v4 (free)
Attached as HEROKU_POSTGRESQL_GOLD_URL
Database has been created and is available
   ! This database is empty. If upgrading, you can transfer
   ! data from another database with pgbackups:restore.
Use `heroku addons:docs heroku-postgresql` to view documentation.
```

Creating the first database

Now you have the **Heroku Postgres** add-on installed in your application and the first database was automatically created by the HEROKU_POSTGRESQL_GOLD_URL environment variable on Heroku and is available; this variable points the connection string to the database.

The name of the HEROKU_POSTGRESQL_GOLD_URL variable follows the pattern HEROKU_POSTGRESQL_[COLOR]_URL, so don't worry if a different name appears.

Heroku allows you to add the **Heroku Postgres** add-on more than once in the same application; it allows you to have many PostgreSQL databases in the same application. In this case, you will have many configuration variables to connect to the database, one for each database.

There is an environment variable called DATABASE_URL; this variable always points to the primary database.

If you want to view all the available environment variables, you must use the following command:

```
$ heroku config --app your-app-name
=== your-app-name Config Vars
DATABASE_URL:                    postgres://username:password@host:5432/
database

HEROKU_POSTGRESQL_GOLD_URL: postgres://username:password@host:5432/
database
```

In this case, you have the DATABASE_URL and HEROKU_POSTGRESQL_GOLD_URL variables that point to the same database connection.

If you visit the Heroku dashboard, you will see the **Heroku Postgres** add-on added in the Hobby Dev plan.

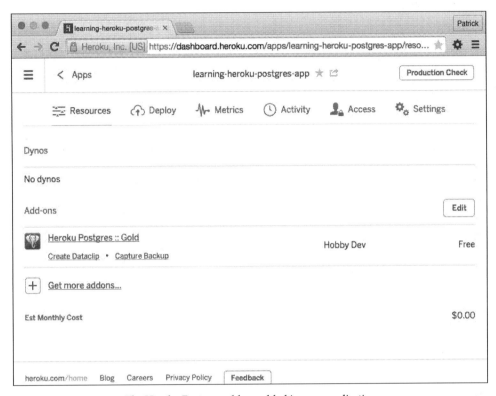

The Heroku Postgres add-on added in your application

Heroku Postgres web interface

Heroku provides a web interface that allows you to view and manage your database. It is available by clicking on the link **Heroku Postgres :: Gold** in the dashboard or visiting the address `https://postgres.heroku.com`.

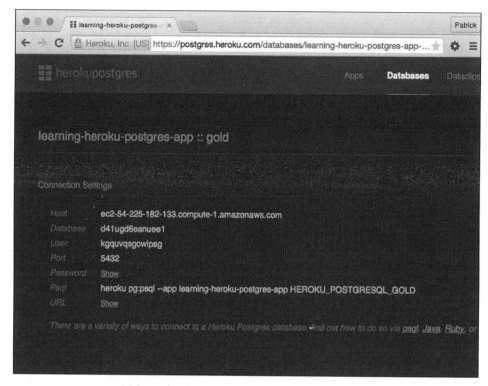

Web interface for managing your PostgreSQL database

In this interface, you have information about the database, such as host, database, user, port, password, how to access `psql`, and other statistics about the database. In addition, you can perform sophisticated tasks that you will learn later in this book.

Using the Heroku client with Postgres

The Heroku Postgres add-on is integrated with the Heroku client, which provides commands that allow you to automate and perform tasks to manage your PostgreSQL database hosted on Heroku.

All these commands are available through the namespace `pg`. You will get an overview of each of these commands in upcoming sections. Open a Terminal and type the following commands.

The pg:info command

This command provides the following statistics and information on your database:

- The connection variable
- The current database plan
- The number of connections
- The PostgreSQL version
- The database's creation date
- The database size
- The number of tables
- The number of available lines if the database plan is Hobby tier

It also informs whether Fork/Follow/Rollback are enabled for this database.

```
$ heroku pg:info --app your-app-name
=== HEROKU_POSTGRESQL_GOLD_URL (DATABASE_URL)
Plan:          Hobby-dev
Status:        Available
Connections:   0
PG Version:    9.3.3
Created:       2014-05-25 14:03 UTC
Data Size:     6.4 MB
Tables:        0
Rows:          0/10000 (In compliance)
Fork/Follow:   Unsupported
Rollback:      Unsupported
```

The pg:psql command

The psql is the PostgreSQL interactive terminal that allows you to type queries interactively as well as see the results. You can also send files to be processed, and provide a number of meta-commands and shell-like features to facilitate script writing and automating tasks.

 You must have PostgreSQL installed on your computer to be able to use this command.

The following command uses the pg:psql command:

```
$ heroku pg:psql --app your-app-name
---> Connecting to HEROKU_POSTGRESQL_GOLD_URL (DATABASE_URL)
psql (9.3.4, server 9.3.3)
SSL connection (cipher: DHE-RSA-AES256-SHA, bits: 256)
Type "help" for help.
your-app-name::GOLD=>
```

For Windows users, `psql` was built to be a console application and by default the Windows Command Prompt uses a different encoding for the rest of the system. When `psql` detects a code page that returns an error, it generates a warning at startup.

To set the correct console code page, two actions are necessary:

First, set the appropriate code page through the command `cmd.exe /c chcp 1252`.

After that, apply the font Lucida Console to the Command Prompt. Right-click on the title bar and select **Properties**, then click on the **Font** tab, and finally select the **Lucida Console** font.

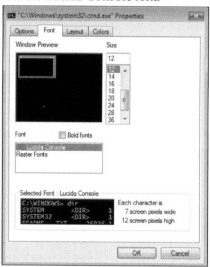

If you have more than one database in your application and want to connect to it, it is necessary to inform the connection variable. By default, the pg:psql command will always connect the main database and set in the DATABASE_URL variable.

```
$ heroku pg:psql HEROKU_POSTGRESQL_[COLOR]_URL --app your-app-name
---> Connecting to HEROKU_POSTGRESQL_[COLOR]_URL
```

```
psql (9.3.4, server 9.3.3)
SSL connection (cipher: DHE-RSA-AES256-SHA, bits: 256)
Type "help" for help.


your-app-name::[COLOR]=>
```

The pg:push command

This command sends the structure and data from a local database your computer to the database application on Heroku. This command expects you to supply the name of your local database and the name of the database on Heroku.

> If your environment is Windows, you must first create the variables that indicate the user and password of PostgreSQL locally. For working on Windows, execute the following commands in the Command Prompt:
>
> ```
> $ SET PGUSER=your_postgres_username_locally
> $ SET PGPASSWORD=your_postgres_password_locally
> ```

```
$ heroku pg:push my_local_database DATABASE_URL --app your-app-name
```

> You must enter the password of your local PostgreSQL if your operating system is Windows. A prompt asking for the password will appear:
>
> ```
> Password: your_postgres_password_locally
> ```

For Linux and Mac OS X, in some cases it is necessary to specify the username and password to access your PostgreSQL locally. In this case, you can proceed in this way:

```
$ PGUSER=your_postgres_username_locally PGPASSWORD=your_postgres_
password_locally heroku pg:push my_local_database DATABASE_URL --app
your-app-name
```

The DATABASE_URL variable is the default database of your application, if you want to send to another database, you must provide the appropriate URL:

```
$ heroku pg:push my_local_database HEROKU_POSTGRESQL_[COLOR]_URL --app
your-app-name
```

The pg:pull command

The pg:pull command copies the structure and data from a database on Heroku to a local database on your computer. This command is useful when you want to analyze data locally or perform tests with an exact copy of the database.

This command expects you to provide the URL of the Heroku database and the name of the new database that will be created on you computer.

```
$ heroku pg:pull DATABASE_URL my_local_database --app your-app-name
```

> You must enter the password of your local PostgreSQL if your operating system is Windows. A prompt asking for the password will appear:
>
> ```
> Password: your_postgres_password_locally
> ```

If the database already exists on your computer, the Heroku client displays a message stating that the database already exists and asks you to delete the database manually before performing pg:pull.

```
$ heroku pg:pull HEROKU_POSTGRESQL_[COLOR]_URL my_local_database --app
your-app-name
! createdb: database creation failed: ERROR:
  database "my_local_database" already exists
! Please drop the local database (`dropdb my_local_database`) and
  try again.
$ dropdb my_local_database
$ heroku pg:pull HEROKU_POSTGRESQL_[COLOR]_URL my_local_database --app
your-app-name
```

Depending on the configuration of PostgreSQL on you computer, it may be necessary in some cases to provide the PostgreSQL username and password so that you'll be able to perform the pg:pull command. In this case, you must provide PGUSER and PGPASSWORD.

For Linux and Mac OS X:

```
$ PGUSER=your_postgres_username_locally PGPASSWORD=your_postgres_
password_locally heroku pg:pull DATABASE_URL
my_local_database --app your-app-name
```

For Windows:

```
$ SET PGUSER=your_postgres_username_locally
$ SET PGPASSWORD=your_postgres_password_locally
$ heroku pg:pull DATABASE_URL
my_local_database --app your-app-name
```

The pg:ps command

The pg:ps command checks the pg_stat_statements table and provides you a concise overview of all the queries that are currently running. It is useful for you to understand how your database is behaving before taking any decision.

```
$ heroku pg:ps --app your-app-name
pid   | state   | source  |running_for       | waiting | query

-----+--------+--------+-----------------+--------+------

26857| active |        | -00:00:00.00103 | f       | SELECT   "doctors".*
FROM "doctors"  ORDER BY name asc LIMIT 1

(1 row)
```

The pg:kill command

This command is used to cancel a query through the process number (pid). You can get this number through the pg:ps command. The command calls the pg_cancel_backend function and tries to cancel the query.

```
$ heroku pg:kill 26857 --app your-app-name

pg_cancel_backend

-------------------

t

(1 row)
```

In some cases, the preceding command may fail. In these cases, you can use the --force parameter that uses the pg_terminate_backend function to bring down the entire connection of the query.

```
$ heroku pg:kill 26857 --force --app your-app-name

pg_terminate_backend

--------------------

t

(1 row)
```

 Use the pg:kill command carefully, so you don't upset your customers.

The pg:killall command

The `pg:killall` command cancels all queries in the database. For this, the `pg_terminate_backend` function is used to bring down the entire connection of each query, is as follows:

```
$ heroku pg:killall --app your-app-name
pg_terminate_backend
---------------------
t
t
(2 rows)
```

The pg:promote command

This command is useful to change the default database in your application. Through it you can change which database responds to the DATABASE_URL variable. This command is used frequently when a problem occurs, and then you can restore the backup in another database and transform it to the default database.

To try this feature, you will add a new database and after that you will promote it to the primary database:

```
$ heroku addons:add heroku-postgresql:hobby-dev -app your-app-name
Adding heroku-postgresql:hobby-dev on your-app-name... done, v17 (free)
Attached as HEROKU_POSTGRESQL_MAROON_URL
Database has been created and is available
 ! This database is empty. If upgrading, you can transfer
 ! data from another database with pgbackups:restore.
Use `heroku addons:docs heroku-postgresql` to view documentation.
```

The command expects you to inform the URL about the database that will be promoted to the DATABASE_URL:

```
$ heroku pg:promote HEROKU_POSTGRESQL_MAROON_URL --app your-app-name
  Promoting HEROKU_POSTGRESQL_MAROON_URL to DATABASE_URL... done
```

You can use the `pg:info` command to check the change in the DATABASE_URL variable:

```
$ heroku pg:info --app your-app-name
=== HEROKU_POSTGRESQL_GOLD_URL
Plan:       Hobby-dev
Status:     Available
```

```
Connections:  0
PG Version:   9.3.3
Created:      2014-05-25 14:03 UTC
Data Size:    6.9 MB
Tables:       9
Rows:         23/10000 (In compliance)
Fork/Follow:  Unsupported
Rollback:     Unsupported


=== HEROKU_POSTGRESQL_MAROON_URL (DATABASE_URL)
Plan:         Hobby-dev
Status:       Available
Connections:  0
PG Version:   9.3.3
Created:      2014-05-25 22:47 UTC
Data Size:    7.1 MB
Tables:       9
Rows:         23/10000 (In compliance)
Fork/Follow:  Unsupported
Rollback:     Unsupported
```

The pg:credentials command

The pg:credentials command supplies access credentials to the database. This command expects you to provide the database URL so that you can get the credentials. The string and connection URL are provided.

```
$ heroku pg:credentials DATABASE_URL --app your-app-name
```

Connection info string:

```
"dbname=dcumcl8ngtuvm host=ec2-54-225-168-181.compute-1.amazonaws.com
  port=5432 user=tzsbkrytsagtxv password=t6W3sUiGL4FebFF6oCqsUs4PeV
sslmode=require"
```

Connection URL:

```
postgres://tzsbkrytsagtxv:t6W3sUiGL4FebFF6oCqsUs4PeV@ec2-54-225-168-
  181.compute-1.amazonaws.com:5432/dcumcl8ngtuvm
```

In some situations, you may need to change the access credentials, you can do this by adding the `--reset` parameter, and then a new username and password will be generated for the database connection.

```
$ heroku pg:credentials DATABASE_URL --reset --app your-app-name
Resetting credentials for HEROKU_POSTGRESQL_[COLOR]_URL (DATABASE_URL)...
done

Promoting HEROKU_POSTGRESQL_[COLOR]_URL (DATABASE_URL)... done
```

Finally, you can enter the `pg:credentials` command again to get the new connection credentials:

```
$ heroku pg:credentials DATABASE_URL --app your-app-name
Connection info string:

"dbname=dcumcl8ngtuvm host=ec2-54-225-168-181.compute-1.amazonaws.
com port=5432 user=fodmwtkpudycuq password=wU-H4j2eMhjYUJk7M61FvSgl33
sslmode=require"

Connection URL:

postgres://fodmwtkpudycuq:wU-H4j2eMhjYUJk7M61FvSgl33@ec2-54-225-168-
   181.compute-1.amazonaws.com:5432/dcumcl8ngtuvm
```

The pg:reset command

The `pg:reset` command is very useful for recreating your database and leaving it without data. If you try to run the `pg:push` command for a database that already has data, the Heroku client will notify you with the following message:

```
$ heroku pg:push my_local_database HEROKU_POSTGRESQL_[COLOR]_URL --app
your-app-name

!    Remote database is not empty.

!    Please create a new database, or use `heroku pg:reset`
```

This command expects you to provide the specific URL of the database on which you'd like to perform the `pg:reset` command. You can use the DATABASE_URL command for the default database or another URL in the pattern HEROKU_POSTGRESQL_[COLOR]_URL.

```
$ heroku pg:reset HEROKU_POSTGRESQL_[COLOR]_URL --app your-app-name

!    WARNING: Destructive Action

!    This command will affect the app: your-app-name

!    To proceed, type "your-app-name" or re-run this command with
--confirm your-app-name
```

This is a destructive action and Heroku client asks you to confirm the action by typing the application name. Only after this, the `pg:reset` process will succeed.

```
> your-app-name
Resetting HEROKU_POSTGRESQL_[COLOR]_URL... done
```

Connecting with Java

There are many ways to connect to the database using Java, the most common way is through the parameters contained in the database connection URL. It provides you with the information `postgres://[username]:[password]@[host]/[database name]`.

JDBC

You can connect via JDBC using the `DATABASE_URL` variable or using another database URL provided by Heroku. The JDBC connection is performed through the database URL parsing and extracting the necessary parameters. The following is just a code sample to help you understand the concept:

```
URI connectionParams = new URI(System.getenv("DATABASE_URL"));

String jdbcUrl = "jdbc:postgresql://" + connectionParams.getHost() +
connectionParams.getPath();

Properties properties = new Properties();

properties.setProperty("username", connectionParams.getUserInfo().
split(":")[0]);

properties.setProperty("password", connectionParams.getUserInfo().
split(":")[1]);

Connection connection = DriverManager.getConnection(jdbcUrl, properties);
```

Spring/XML

The following code allows Spring XML connection. It configures `BasicDataSource` through the `DATABASE_URL` variable and can be used with Hibernate, JPA, and others. The following is just a code sample to help you understand the concept:

```
<bean class="java.net.URI" id="connectionParams">

    <constructor-arg value="#{systemEnvironment['DATABASE_URL']}"/>

</bean>

<bean class="org.apache.commons.dbcp.BasicDataSource" destroy-
method="close" id="dataSource">
```

```
    <property name="driverClassName" value="org.postgresql.Driver" />

    <property name="username" value="#{@connectionParams.getUserInfo().
split(':')[0]}" />

    <property name="password" value="#{@connectionParams.getUserInfo().
split(':')[1]}" />

    <property name="url" value="#{'jdbc:postgresql://' + @
connectionParams.getHost() + @connectionParams.getPath()}" />

</bean>
```

Connecting with Ruby

In order to use PostgreSQL as a database in Ruby applications, it is necessary to install `gem pg` in your `Gemfile`.

```
gem 'pg'
```

After that, run the `bundle install` command to download and install the necessary dependencies.

For applications in Ruby on Rails, it is not necessary to configure the database connection. When Heroku deploys your application, it automatically configures the `database.yml` file through the DATABASE_URL environment variable.

Connecting with Python

In order to use PostgreSQL as database in your Python applications it is necessary to use the `psycopg2` package and add it in the dependency file called `requirements.txt`. The following is just a code sample to help you understand the concept;

```
$ pip install psycopg2
$ pip freeze > requirements.txt
```

Then, use the `psycopg2` package to connect the DATABASE_URL variable:

```
import psycopg2
import urlparse
import os


try:
    urlparse.uses_netloc.append("postgres")
    connection_params = urlparse.urlparse(os.environ["DATABASE_URL"])
```

```
    db_connection = psycopg2.connect(database = connection_params.
path[1:], user = connection_params.username, password = connection_
params.password, host = connection_params.hostname, port = connection_
params.port)

except:
    print "Database connection failed."
```

Connecting with Django

To connect to PostgreSQL using the Django framework it is necessary to install the dj-database-url package and add it in the dependency file called requirements.txt.

```
$ pip install dj-database-url
$ pip freeze > requirements.txt
```

Then add the following code at the bottom of settings.py file:

```
import dj_database_url
DATABASES['default'] = dj_database_url.config()
```

In the deploy process, the DATABASE_URL variable will be parsed and converted into a form that Django can understand.

Connecting with Node.js

In order to connect to PostgreSQL with Node.js it is necessary to use the pg module. To make that possible, you have to add it to the dependency file called package.json. The following is just a code sample to help you understand the concept:

```
"dependencies": {
"pg": "0.10.2",
"express": "latest"
}
```

Then use the pg module to connect to PostgreSQL through the DATABASE_URL environment variable in your code:

```
var pg = require('pg');
pg.connect(process.env.DATABASE_URL, function(err, client, done) {
  if(err) {
    return console.error('Client error.', err);
  }
```

```
client.query('SELECT * FROM doctors', function(err, result) {
  done();

  if(err) {
    return console.error('Query error.', err);
  }

  console.log(result.rows);
});
});
```

Connection permissions

When a database is created, the Heroku Postgres add-on grants all non-superuser permissions in your database; you can use SELECT, INSERT, UPDATE, DELETE, TRUNCATE, REFERENCES, TRIGGER, CREATE, CONNECT, TEMPORARY, EXECUTE, and USAGE.

You cannot create or modify database roles, because you don't have superuser permissions.

Multiple schemas

Another important point is the use of multiple schemas. Heroku Postgres doesn't limit the amount of schemas, so you can use the desired amount.

You must use the schemas in a careful way. In database instances with more than 50 schemas, a performance loss can occur in the tool's database snapshots and PG Backups.

External connections

Heroku Postgres allows you to use client software to access your database. All connections require you to use SSL. The client software used is often interesting, especially when you want to run a query using a friendlier interface.

To be able to perform the connection, you need the following connection data: the database name, host, port, user, and password. You can get this data through the `pg:credentials` command:

```
$ heroku pg:credentials DATABASE_URL --app your-app-name
```

Connection info string:

```
"dbname=dcumcl8ngtuvm host=ec2-54-225-168-181.compute-1.amazonaws.
com port=5432 user=fodmwtkpudycuq password=wU-H4j2eMhjYUJk7M61FvSg133
sslmode=require"
```

Connection URL:

```
postgres://fodmwtkpudycuq:wU-H4j2eMhjYUJk7M61FvSg133@ec2-54-225-168-181.
compute-1.amazonaws.com:5432/dcumcl8ngtuvm
```

Through the data contained in the `connection info string`, you can use pgAdmin to connect to your database. Click on the **File** menu, then on **Add Server...** and fill the fields with the data connection details:

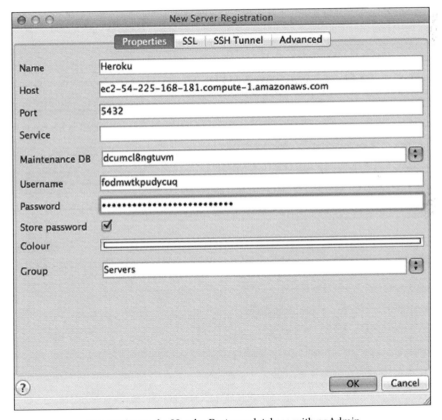

Connecting to the Heroku Postgres database with pgAdmin

Connecting to databases from outside Heroku

In some cases, you may want your application to connect to a database that isn't hosted in Heroku. You can configure this connection by overriding the DATABASE_ URL command.

To override this variable, you must provide the connection parameters:

```
postgres://[username]:[password]@[host]/[database name]
```

The Heroku client has the config:set command that allows you to define or override environment variables:

```
$ heroku config:set DATABASE_URL=' postgres://[username]:[password]@
[host]/[database name]' -your-app-name
Setting config vars and restarting your-app-name... done, v11
DATABASE_URL: postgres://[username]:[password] @[host]:5432/
   [database name]
```

Monitoring and logging

Logs are important to understand the behavior of your application and to identify problems. Heroku also offers, through its client, a way to track the logs generated:

```
$ heroku logs -t --app your-app-name
2014-05-25T13:16:09.958885+00:00 heroku[api]: Enable Logplex by
patrickespake@gmail.com
2014-05-25T13:16:09.958885+00:00 heroku[api]: Release v2 created by
   patrickespake@gmail.com
```

You can apply a filter in the command logs to view only the logs generated by PostgreSQL using the -p postgres flag:

```
$ heroku logs -p postgres -t --app your-app-name
```

To see all the options provided by the command logs, you can use the --help flag:

```
$ heroku logs --help
```

```
Usage: heroku logs

display recent log output

-n, --num NUM          # the number of lines to display
-p, --ps PS            # only display logs from the given process
-s, --source SOURCE    # only display logs from the given source
-t, --tail             # continually stream logs
```

 Chapter 7, Understanding Log Statements and Common Errors covers more information about Heroku's log system.

Removing the add-on

The most common way to remove the Heroku Postgres add-on is through the Heroku client using the environment variable in the pattern HEROKU_POSTGRESQL_ [COLOR]_URL:

```
$ heroku addons:remove HEROKU_POSTGRESQL_[COLOR]_URL --app
  your-app-name


!    WARNING: Destructive Action

!    This command will affect the app: your-app-name

!    To proceed, type "your-app-name" or re-run this command with
       --confirm your-app-name


> your-app-name
Removing HEROKU_POSTGRESQL_[COLOR] on your-app-name... done, v19
  (free)
```

In order to confirm the deletion, you must enter the application name.

It's also possible to delete the Heroku Postgres add-on through the Heroku dashboard. For that, access your application via `https://dashboard.heroku.com/apps`. Choose your application and click on the **Edit** button on the right; after that, click on the minus sign and finally click on **Save**.

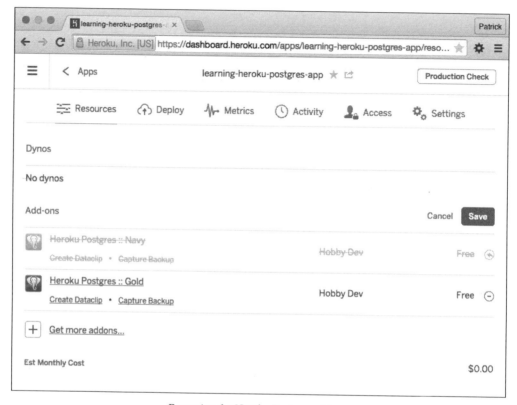

Removing the Heroku Postgres add-on

Self-test Questions

Answer true or false:

1. Does Heroku allow duplicate application names?

2. Is it possible to create an application via the Heroku Client and Heroku dashboard?

3. Is the Heroku Postgres add-on available to install the add-ons page gallery?

4. When the Heroku Postgres add-on is installed, is it necessary to manually create the first database?

5. Does the DATABASE_URL variable contain information regarding the database connection?

6. Does the Heroku Client provide commands to work with PostgreSQL?

7. Is it possible to copy the Heroku database through the heroku pg:pull command?

8. Is the heroku pg:promote command helpful to define the main database?

9. Does the Heroku Postgres add-on not allow connection with programing languages such as Java, Ruby, Python, and Node.js?

10. Does Heroku Postgres allow multiple schemas in the database?

Summary

In this chapter, you learned how to configure your local environment to work with PostgreSQL and pgAdmin. Besides that, you have also understood how to install Heroku Postgres in your application.

In addition, you have understood that the first database is created automatically when the Heroku Postgres add-on is installed in your application and there are several PostgreSQL databases as well. You also learned that the great majority of tasks can be performed in two ways: via the Heroku Client and via the Heroku dashboard.

You have also learned that Heroku Client is a very powerful tool to work with PostgreSQL; it provides a set of useful commands such as pg:info, pg:psql, pg:push, pg:pull, pg:ps, pg:kill, pg:killall, pg:promote, pg:credentials, and pg:reset.

You also looked at how to connect to your PostgreSQL database using programming and frameworks supported by Heroku, and learned how to connect to your database using pgAdmin.

Finally, you learned how to use a database that isn't hosted on Heroku application, and about monitoring, information logging, and removing the Heroku Postgres add-on.

In the next chapter, we will learn about backups, how to generate backups, and importing and exporting databases. In addition, you will also learn about data security and how to upgrade databases.

4
PG Backups

Backups are important at any level. Failures are possible to occur at any system that uses the database. It may be an accidental failure, data corruption, or hardware-related. You need to perform actions anticipating failures and take steps to ensure data integrity. Therefore, Heroku offers an add-on called **PG Backups** that allows you to create and restore backups of your Postgres database hosted on Heroku, and also to import and export data.

In this chapter, you will learn how to use the features that this add-on provides.

This chapter will cover the following topics:

- Plans
- Installing the add-on
- Changing the plan
- Creating a backup
- Listing backups
- Downloading a backup
- Deleting backups
- Restoring from a backup
- Importing databases
- Exporting databases
- Removing the add-on

Plans

Before installing the **PG Backups** add-on, it is important to understand the plans offered and identify which one is the best for your application.

Currently, the add-on provides three different plans; all of them are free and the main difference is the period of data retention.

The **Plus** plan is recommended if you want to generate backups manually or in automated routines. This plan isn't recommended for new users as the responsibility for creating backups is yours. The **Auto – One Week Retention** and **Auto – One Month Retention** plans will create automated backups weekly or monthly, and you don't need do anything in order to make it happen.

In the following table you can compare the plans offered:

Plan	Manual backups retained	Weekly backups retained	Daily backups retained	Automatic daily backups	Intended for databases up to 20 GB
Plus	7	0	0	Unavailable	Yes
Auto – One Month Retention	2	5	7	Available	Yes
Auto – One Week Retention	2	0	7	Available	Yes

Plans

 For new users, it is recommended to use the **Auto - One Month Retention** plan. This plan offers one month of data retention.

All the plans that are offered are available at https://addons.heroku.com/pgbackups.

Installing the add-on

After choosing the plan that suits you best, you can install the add-on in your Heroku application. This installation can be done in two different ways: via the Heroku client and via the web interface.

The PG Backups add-on is free with all plans, but Heroku requires that you enter your credit card information to install the add-on. For this visit the URL `https://dashboard.heroku.com/account/billing`.

Via the Heroku client

The command to install via the Heroku client will depend on the chosen plan. For the **Plus** plan, you should enter the following command in your operating system Terminal:

```
$ heroku addons:add pgbackups --app your-app-name
Adding pgbackups on your-app-name... done, v22 (free)
You can now use "pgbackups" to backup your databases or import an
external backup.
Use `heroku addons:docs pgbackups` to view documentation.
```

For the **Auto – One Month Retention** plan, enter the following command:

```
$ heroku addons:add pgbackups:auto-month --app your-app-name
Adding pgbackups:auto-month on your-app-name... done, v24 (free)
You can now use "pgbackups" to backup your databases or import an
external backup.
Use `heroku addons:docs pgbackups` to view documentation.
```

And finally, for the **Auto – One Week Retention** plan, enter the following command:

```
$ heroku addons:add pgbackups:auto-week --app your-app-name
Adding pgbackups:auto-week on your-app-name... done, v26 (free)
You can now use "pgbackups" to backup your databases or import an
external backup.
Use `heroku addons:docs pgbackups` to view documentation.
```

Basically, the difference between the commands is just the kind of plan used: pgbackups, pgbackups:auto-month, or pgbackups:auto-week.

Via the web interface

To install via the web interface, you must access the **PG Backups** add-ons page at `https://addons.heroku.com/pgbackups`. Choose the best plan for you; at the bottom of the page select the app name and click on the **Add [Plan Name] for Free** button.

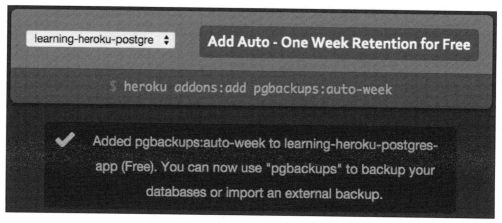

Installing the PG Backups add-on via the web interface

 A confirmation message will appear informing you whether the installation was successful.

Changing the plan

The **PG Backups** add-on allows you to change the type of plan whenever it's more convenient for you. This way you can easily change the retention period of your backups: for weekly, monthly, or focusing more on manual backups.

To do this, visit the dashboard of your application in `https://dashboard.heroku.com/apps`, click on the **Edit** button, select the plan you want to change beside the **PG Backups** add-on, and click on the **Save** button to confirm.

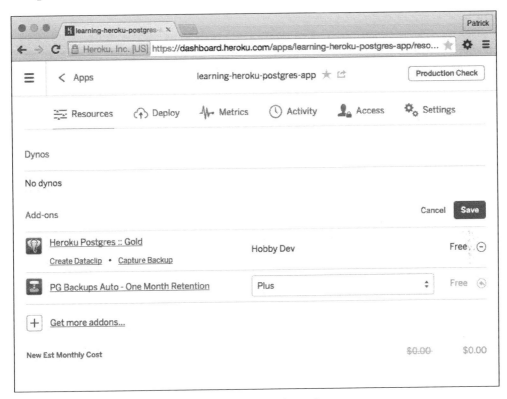

Changing the PG Backups plan

Creating a backup

By default, **PG Backups** take backups of your primary database, available via the `DATABASE_URL` configuration variable.

To generate a new backup, you must enter the command manually:

```
$ heroku pgbackups:capture --app your-app-name
HEROKU_POSTGRESQL_COBALT_URL (DATABASE_URL)   ----backup---> b002
Capturing... done
Storing... done
```

Backups are always compressed, and are always smaller than the size of your database.

If you have another database in your app, you can specify the database to take the back up through this configuration variable:

```
$ heroku pgbackups:capture HEROKU_POSTGRESQL_[COLOR]_URL --app
  your-app-name
```

 Automated backups are always performed on the primary database, available via the DATABASE_URL configuration variable.

Each plan has a limit for manual backups, so, if you have already reached this limit, you will need to delete the previous backup so that you can take a new manual backup. You can do it through the `--expire` flag:

```
$ heroku pgbackups:capture --expire --app your-app-name
```

There is another way to perform backups; you can take backups through the GUI (graphical user interface) provided to manage your Postgres databases in https://postgres.heroku.com/databases. For this, click on the name of your database; after this, click on the gear icon on the right-hand side and select the **New Snapshot** option.

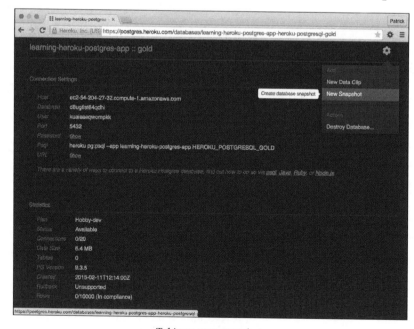

Taking a new snapshot

The backup process adds overhead to your database during the process. This overhead can vary according to the size of your database, but it doesn't block other operations on the database while a backup is ongoing. In *Chapter 6, Rollback, Followers, and Forks*, you will learn another way to improve this process through the use of followers.

Listing backups

There are two ways to view a list of backups; the first one is via the Heroku client and the second is via the web interface. The information provided is the backup ID and also the data, status, size, and which database was backed up.

Via the Heroku client

To see a list of backups via the Heroku client, you must enter the following command:

```
$ heroku pgbackups --app your-app-name
```

> Backups with an ID starting with the letter a are automatic backups and backups starting with the letter b are manual backups.

Via the web interface

To view a list of backups via the web interface, you must access `https://postgres.heroku.com`. Click on the database name and, at the bottom of the page, you will find information about all the existing backups.

Backups listed

> In this interface, the backups are called snapshots.

Downloading a backup

Downloading backups is a very common action when you want to migrate data between applications, upgrade plans, or simply export data.

The simplest way to download a backup is via the web interface at Heroku Postgres in `https://postgres.heroku.com`. In the backup list, there is a link to download each backup, but it's also very common to download the backup via the Heroku client with the `pgbackups:url` command:

```
$ heroku pgbackups:url --app your-app-name
```

```
"https://s3.amazonaws.com/hkpgbackups/app25633057@heroku.com/b004.dump?AW
SAccessKeyId=AKIAJNFEZJDWEFCGIL7A&Expires=1406498011&Signature=fICrkAEAQU
xClStvBKgMM%2FspYkI%3D"
```

This command will always provide the appropriate URL to download the most recent backup. If you want another backup, you can pass the `backup ID`:

```
$ heroku pgbackups:url b002 --app your-app-name
```

And finally, to download you can use commands such as `curl` or `wget` with the `pgbackups:url` command:

```
$ curl -o latest.dump `heroku pgbackups:url --app your-app-name`
```

Deleting backups

Similar to downloading backups, you can also delete backups via the web interface at Heroku Postgres `https://postgres.heroku.com`. Select a database and click on the **Delete** link in the list.

You can delete a backup via the client through the `pgbackups:destroy` command. This command expects you to pass the `backup ID` to perform the deletion:

```
$ heroku pgbackups:destroy b004 --app your-app-name
Destroying b004... done
```

Restoring from a backup

The backup restore process is a destructive operation. The existing data is deleted and replaced with the data in the backup. You can do this process via the Heroku client through the `pgbackups:restore` command. It expects you to enter the database configuration variable and the `backup ID` to perform the restore:

```
$ heroku pgbackups:restore DATABASE_URL a001 --app your-app-name
```

```
HEROKU_POSTGRESQL_COBALT_URL (DATABASE_URL)   <---restore---   a001
DATABASE_URL
2014/07/27 04:21.28 +0000
1.4KB
! WARNING: Destructive Action
! This command will affect the app: your-app-name
!   To proceed, type " your-app-name " or re-run this command with
--confirm your-app-name
> your-app-name
Retrieving... done
Restoring... done
```

 This is a destructive action; you are prompted to enter the name of your app to confirm the process.

Importing databases

You can use the **PG Backups** add-on to import database dumps from other databases to your Heroku Postgres database. This can be done using the `pgbackups:restore` command through a dump database generated by the `pg_dump` tool.

 If your environment is Windows, you must first create the variables that indicate the user and password of PostgreSQL locally. For working on Windows, execute the following commands in the Command Prompt:

```
SET PGUSER=your_postgres_username_locally
SET PGPASSWORD=your_postgres_password_locally
```

The `pg_dump` tool is present by default in the PostgreSQL installation on your computer or other web servers. To generate a new dump, you must enter this command for Linux and Mac OS X:

```
$ PGPASSWORD=your-db-password pg_dump -Fc --no-acl --no-owner -h
  localhost -U your-db-username your-database-name > mydb.dump
```

For Window users, enter the following command:

```
$ pg_dump -Fc --no-acl --no-owner -h
  localhost -U your-db-username your-database-name > mydb.dump
```

Importing in Heroku Postgres

To import the dump of your database to Heroku, the first step is to upload the file somewhere accessible via an HTTP URL; after that, you can restore the backup through the pgbackups:restore command:

```
$ heroku pgbackups:restore DATABASE_URL
  'http://your-server.com/mydb.dump' --app your-app-name
```

 You have to add the dump file on your website and include the URL in the preceding command. It is highly recommended to remove the dump file generated after the backup restore.

Exporting databases

Exporting a database from Heroku Postgres and restoring it on your computer or on another server is a simple process. The first step is to generate a new backup, download it, and finally restore the backup using the pg_restore tool.

Downloading the backup

As you learned earlier, it's possible to generate a new backup and download it:

```
$ heroku pgbackups:capture --app your-app-name
$ curl -o latest.dump `heroku pgbackups:url --app your-app-name`
```

Restoring to local database

A restore operation uses the pg_restore tool. It is installed by default during the PostgreSQL installation locally. For restoring the database, enter the following command:

```
$ pg_restore --verbose --clean --no-acl --no-owner -h
  localhost -U your-db-username -d your-database-name latest.dump
```

Removing the add-on

Removing an add-on should always be done with great care, especially in the case of the **PG Backups** add-on as all backups are deleted after being excluded. So it is recommended that you download or restore backups before performing this action.

As with the installation, it is possible to remove the add-on in two different ways: via the Heroku client or via the web interface. You can choose which ever method is more convenient for you.

Via the Heroku client

Irrespective of the selected plan, you can remove the **PG Backups** add-on with one command:

```
$ heroku addons:remove pgbackups --app your-app-name
! WARNING: Destructive Action
! This command will affect the app: your-heroku-app-name
!   To proceed, type " your-app-name " or re-run this command with
--confirm your-app-name
> your-app-name
Removing pgbackups on your-heroku-app-name... done, v27 (free)
```

 This is a destructive action, so you are prompted to enter the name of your app to confirm the process.

Via the web interface

Actions via the web interface are the favorite of new users in the Heroku platform, although not all actions can be performed via the web interface.

The add-on removal is a functionality available and commonly used via the GUI in Heroku. For this, visit your app dashboard at `https://dashboard.heroku.com/apps/`, select the application, click on the **Edit** button, click on the – (less) button beside the name of the **PG Backups** add-on, and confirm the deletion by clicking on the **Save** button.

Self-test Questions

Answer true or false:

1. Is it only possible to do automated backups on Heroku via the **PG Backups** add-on?

2. Are the backups done by default on the primary database, available via the `DATABASE_URL` configuration variable?

3. Are all PG Backups plans paid?

4. Can you download a backup via the web interface?

5. Are you only able to delete backups via the client?

6. Is the `heroku pgbackups:restore` command used to restore backups?

7. Is the `heroku pgbackups:url` command used to change the URL connection to the database?

8. Isn't it possible to restore a Heroku Postgres database locally?

9. Can you remove the PG Backups add-on at any time?

10. When the Heroku Postgres add-on is removed, are the backups kept?

Summary

In this chapter, you learned the differences between PG Backups add-on plans and learned how to choose the best plan according to your need, how to use the main features provided by the add-on in order to create backups, and perform a database restore. In addition, you learned how to import database to Heroku and how to export your Heroku Postgres database.

Backup routines are important for the safety and integrity of your data; always remember to configure backups according to your need as failures can occur in any project.

In the next chapter, you will learn how to use Dataclips. Basically, this function allows you to write queries in SQL and share the results with your colleagues; they are able to view the data and download it in many formats. Besides that, you will also learn about security and some limitations.

5

Dataclips

Dataclips are web tool provided by Heroku that allows you to share the results of your queries in a Postgres database in a simple way. You can share the URL of the results with anyone, and they can view or download the results in JSON, CSV, or Microsoft Excel formats.

Heroku dataclips also provide an API end point, which is an amazing feature that quickly creates prototyping APIs. Another use case of dataclips is when you use them for decision-making in your business. With dataclips, it is very easy for someone to share an important business query with you, and you are able to edit and work together on this query or just download the query data. It's a great feature to create dashboards in your applications.

This chapter covers the following topics:

- Creating dataclips
- Sharing dataclips
- Interacting with dataclips
- Dataclips security
- Limitations and additional settings

Creating dataclips

In order to create a dataclip, it is necessary to access `https://dataclips.heroku.com`; this provides a web tool that allows you to create and manage your dataclips.

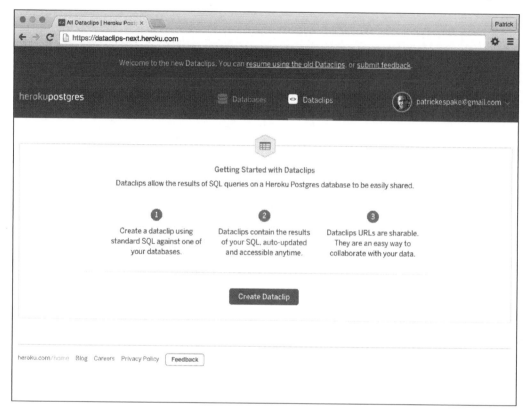

The Heroku dataclips web tool

To create a new dataclip, you should follow these steps:

1. First, click on the **Create Dataclip** button.
2. Then, on the next screen, enter the name of your dataclip, choose the database, and type the SQL query that returns the desired results.
3. Finally, click on the **Create Dataclip** button.

You can use the SELECT * FROM pg_catalog.pg_tables ORDER BY tablename ASC LIMIT 5 query if you don't have data in your database. This query returns the name of the first five tables of your database in an ascending order.

The following screenshot shows the first five tables of pg_tables:

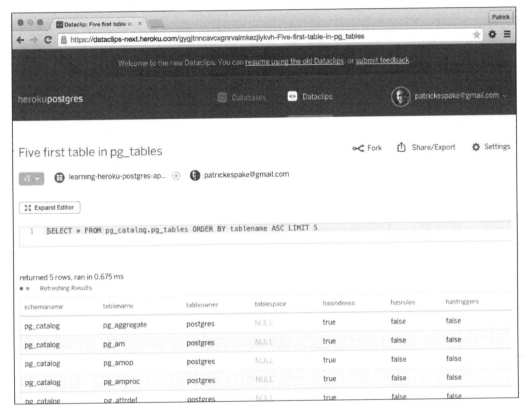

The first five tables in pg_tables

You can change your SQL query at any time. To do this, just change your query and click on the **Update Query** button.

Every time you change the query, a new version is automatically created, and you can easily navigate between versions by clicking on the version button and then on the **View** button in the previous version window.

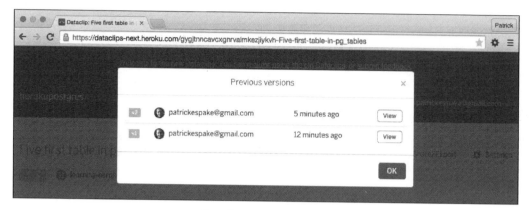

Dataclips previous versions

Sharing dataclips

You can share your dataclips in many different ways; some of them are mentioned here:

- Using the dataclip access link
- Downloading the dataclip in XLS, CSV, or JSON format
- Sending the dataclip access link via Twitter
- Embedding the dataclip via Google Drive

Click on the **Share/Export** link and choose the most suitable way for you, which is shown in the following screenshot:

Share dataclips

Interacting with dataclips

The people with whom you share your dataclip can interact with it directly through the access link. This link allows your dataclip to be seen in the web format and also in the CSV, JSON, or XLS formats.

For example, you can visit a dataclip sample at `https://dataclips-next.heroku.com/gygjtnncavcxgnrvalmkezjiykvh-Five-first-table-in-pg_tables`. The web interface is provided to view the dataclip, and by adding the `.csv`, `.json`, or `.xls` file format, you can view the data in the following formats:

- To view in CSV, go to `https://dataclips-next.heroku.com/gygjtnncavcxgnrvalmkezjiykvh-Five-first-table-in-pg_tables.csv`

- Viewing in JSON: `https://dataclips-next.heroku.com/gygjtnncavcxgnrvalmkezjiykvh-Five-first-table-in-pg_tables.json`

- Viewing in XLS: `https://dataclips-next.heroku.com/gygjtnncavcxgnrvalmkezjiykvh-Five-first-table-in-pg_tables.xls`

If there is more than one available version, you can specify the version by adding the `?version=` parameter. Here is an example:

```
https://dataclips-next.heroku.com/gygjtnncavcxgnrvalmkezjiykvh-Five-
first-table-in-pg_tables.json?version=2
```

 The JSON endpoint is useful for prototyping APIs, but it should not be a substitute for a production API. This endpoint also supports **Cross-Origin Resource Sharing** (**CORS**) for GET requests.

Data refresh

The data visualization of dataclips is never static; it always displays the updated set of data that corresponds to the query, and you are alerted if there is a new set of data.

If your dataclip is connected with Google Drive, the data is updated on an hourly basis.

Dataclips security

All dataclips are secured through an unguessable URL. Heroku also allows only selected users to view your dataclip; this is done by adding the user e-mail in the dataclip's configuration. This functionality is only available on the Standard tier, Premium tier, or Enterprise tier plan.

In order to set the display only for selected users, you must click on the **Settings** link. Then, in the **Security Permissions** section, choose the **Only to authorized users** option. After that, add the e-mails that you want to allow, and finally, click on the **Save Permissions** button:

Dataclip available only to authorized users

When someone accesses the URL of your dataclip, they will be informed that the dataclip is protected and that the user is required to log in to view the results:

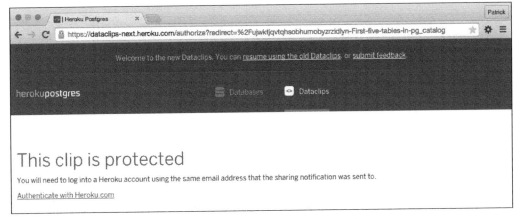

The user must log in to view the results of the dataclip

Limitations and additional settings

Dataclips have some limitations, which are as follows:

- By default, queries that take longer than 10 minutes are canceled
- The query can return a maximum of 29,999 lines
- You can only add authentication in the Standard tier, Premium tier, or Enterprise tier plan

There are some other settings that you can make in your dataclip by clicking on the **Settings** link; these settings are as follows:

- **Rename Dataclip**: This allows you to rename the dataclip.
- **Change Database**: This allows you to move the dataclip query to another database.
- **Remove Dataclip**: This allows you to delete the dataclip. This action makes the dataclip inaccessible.

 There is one more feature available in the dataclip dashboard and accessible through the **Fork Clip** link. This feature allows you to make a copy of dataclip, and it is a useful feature when you want to work on a new version.

Self-test questions

Answer true or false:

1. Can dataclips' queries in Postgres database on Heroku be shared?
2. Can dataclips be displayed in the browser?
3. Is it possible to download a dataclip in the XLS format?
4. To create a dataclip, is it necessary to access `https://dataclips.heroku.com`?
5. Are dataclips recommended for API prototyping?
6. Can you see the results in the JSON format when adding `.json` to the dataclip URL?
7. Are dataclips that are shared on Google Drive never updated?
8. Can dataclips return an infinite set of lines?
9. Can you switch the dataclip to another Postgres database at any time?
10. Is fork a nice feature when you want to make a copy of a dataclip?

Summary

In this chapter, you learned how to use the dataclips tool provided by Heroku. This tool allows you to build SQL queries using a Postgres database hosted on Heroku. You also learned that through dataclips, you can share the results with other people, and they can see the results in many different ways, that is, on the web, in the JSON, CSV, or Microsoft Excel (XLS) formats, and you can embed or share them on Google Drive.

You also saw that dataclips are an interesting feature when working on prototyping APIs, but they should not be used in production APIs.

In the next chapter, you will learn about the rollback, followers, and forks features. Besides this, you will also study some use cases.

6

Rollback, Followers, and Forks

In this chapter, you will learn important concepts related to security, stability, and experiments in the PostgreSQL database on the Heroku platform. We will discuss topics related to rollback, follower databases, and fork databases. These functionalities offered by Heroku Postgres are very useful to ensure the secure storage of your data and the scalability of your Postgres database.

Basically, rollback is related to recovering a prior version of your database and restoring the data and structure of your database. Rollback is a useful feature when your database is corrupted.

A follower database is an essential feature when your concern is scalability and security of your data. A follower database is a replica of your main database in read-only mode; this replica is synchronized automatically on the Heroku infrastructure. You can have as many follower databases as necessary for your application.

Finally, the fork database is useful to test and simulate your application with different versions of the database. The fork database is a copy of the data and the structure of the main database at a specific time.

Throughout this chapter, you will learn how to use each of these features and how to benefit from their functionalities.

In this chapter, we will be cover:

- Heroku Postgres rollback
- Heroku Postgres follower databases
- Heroku Postgres forking databases

Heroku Postgres rollback

The most common use case of rollback is when your database breaks down with a problem after a new push to production. Through the rollback feature, you can roll your database back to before the issue occurred. Another use case is when data loss occurs accidentally in the database. This feature allows database data to be recovered for any given time period.

In *Chapter 4, PG Backups* you learned about PG Backups. It is a great solution for ensuring the security and integrity of your database. Sometimes, people get confused about PG Backups and Heroku Postgres rollback; in fact, they are complementary solutions. Through Heroku Postgres rollback, you have another way to recover your data and maintain the integrity of your database; you can specify the exact period to the rollback.

Checking the rollback feature

The first step for performing rollback is to check whether this feature is available in your plan. Currently, the rollback functionality is available only in standard, premium, and enterprise plans.

You can check whether the rollback is enabled in two different ways. The first one is through the Heroku client with the `heroku pg:info` command:

```
$ heroku pg:info --app your-app-name
=== HEROKU_POSTGRESQL_CHARCOAL_URL (DATABASE_URL)
...

Rollback:      earliest from 2014-10-04 22:56 UTC
...
```

The preceding command displays the rollback information; this tells you whether the feature is available for your database. If the line displays a date, as the one in the preceding command, this means that the feature is available. If the line displays "Unsupported", this means that it is unavailable, as shown here:

```
=== HEROKU_POSTGRESQL_ORANGE_URL (DATABASE_URL)
...

Rollback:      Unsupported
...
```

The second way to check whether rollback is active is through the Heroku Dashboard. Just visit `https://postgres.heroku.com`, select your database, and take a look at the **Statistics** section to check whether the rollback feature is enabled, as shown in the following image:

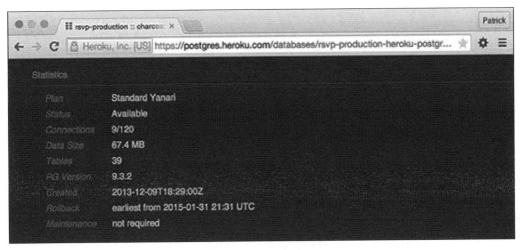

The rollback feature is enabled

Available period

The period available for rollback varies according to your database plan. It is important because it allows you to perform the rollback within the available range. This table shows the periods for each plan:

Heroku Postgres tier	Rollback
Hobby	No
Standard	1 hour
Premium	1 week
Enterprise	1 month

Creating a rollback database

The rollback process consists of the creation of another database with the desired rollback period. Thus, when the rollback is done, it doesn't affect your main database. If you want to change the main database, you need to promote the rollback database. You will see this a little later in the chapter.

To perform a rollback, it is necessary to use the Heroku client. The command consists of the addition of a new database and the `--rollback` flag with the database color name for which the rollback should be done, and you must use the `--to` flag to specify the period of the rollback.

You can specify the time period in two different ways, either using a `2014-10-05 15:02:00+00` timestamp or using the time with the time zone as `2014-10-05 15:02 US/Pacific`.

Thus, the basic command to rollback is as follows:

```
$ heroku addons:add heroku-postgresql:standard-0 --rollback database_
color_name   --to '2014-10-05 15:02:00+00' --app your-app-name
Adding heroku-postgresql:standard-0 on your-app-name... done, v240 ($50/
mo)
Attached as HEROKU_POSTGRESQL_RED_URL
Database will become available after it completes rolling back to 2014-
10-05 15:02:00 +0000 (00:59:43 ago)
Use `heroku pg:wait` to track status.
Use `heroku addons:docs heroku-postgresql` to view documentation.
```

The time to create the rollback database can vary according to the size of your database. You can use the `heroku pg:wait` command to see the progress:

```
$ heroku pg:wait --app your-app-name
Waiting for database HEROKU_POSTGRESQL_RED_URL... \ preparing (5%
  completed)
```

There is another way to perform the rollback. It is through the `--by` flag. You can specify a time interval, and it should be of the `X days X hours X minutes` format. Here is an example:

```
$ heroku addons:add heroku-postgresql:standard-0 --rollback
  database_color_name --by '2 days 5 hours 10 minutes' --app
    your-app-name
```

You cannot specify both the `--by` and `--to` options for rollback. You should specify one or the other.

Promote a rollback database

In some cases, you may want to promote the rollback database to the primary database. You must use the `heroku pg:promote` command with the database color URL to be promoted:

```
$ heroku pg:promote HEROKU_POSTGRESQL_[COLOR]_URL --app your-app-name
```

Deprovisioning a rollback database

At any time, it's possible to remove the rollback database through the `heroku addons:remove` command by passing as parameter the database color URL that you want to remove:

```
$ heroku addons:remove HEROKU_POSTGRESQL_[COLOR]_URL --app your-app-name
```

Heroku Postgres follower databases

The follower database is a feature that helps the scalability of your Heroku applications.

Through the follower database, Heroku provides a way to increase the efficiency of reading your database data by creating a master-slave structure. Each slave is one follower in read-only mode, and the data is updated from master to slave in real time.

The most common use of a follower database is when you want to increase the performance to access your data; for example, imagine that you have a web application with a huge number of users. If all users access the same database, you will probably have performance issues. A good solution to this is to create copies of your main database, and when each user needs any data, the system redirects the request for a copy of the database. This way, you have a database distributed system. Through Heroku Postgres follower databases, you can add many follower databases for your application.

Creating and managing follower databases

The follower feature is enabled for the plans in the standard, premium, and enterprise tiers. You can check whether your database is enabled to use followers through the `heroku pg:info` command:

```
$ heroku pg:info --app your-app-name
=== HEROKU_POSTGRESQL_CHARCOAL_URL (DATABASE_URL)
```

```
...
Fork/Follow: Available
...
```

A follower database must be created from a database that allows us to read and write. Usually, the follower database is created from DATABASE_URL. You cannot create followers in cascade from another follower database.

The creation of a follower database consists of adding a new database through Heroku add-ons and the use of the --follow flag and the database URL from which the follower must be created:

```
$ heroku addons:add heroku-postgresql:standard-2 --follow HEROKU_
POSTGRESQL_[COLOR]_URL --app your-app-name
Adding heroku-postgresql:standard-2 on your-app-name... done, v245 ($200/
mo)
Attached as HEROKU_POSTGRESQL_BLACK_URL
Follower will become available for read-only queries when up-to-date
Use `heroku pg:wait` to track status.
Use `heroku addons:docs heroku-postgresql` to view documentation.
```

In the preceding command, heroku-postgresql:standard-2 informs us about the type of plan that will be used for the follower database. You can select the plan that best suits you, and through https://addons.heroku.com/heroku-postgresql, you can see all the available plans.

 It's recommended that you either choose a higher plan or one that is able to create a new follower database.

Through the heroku pg:wait command, you can check the creation process of a new follower database:

```
$ heroku pg:wait --app your-app-name
Waiting for database HEROKU_POSTGRESQL_BLACK_URL... | preparing (5%
completed)
```

The creation time of a new follower database depends on the size of your database and the use of the database at that time.

Unfollow the main database

You can stop following the main database at anytime. This action does not remove the follower database; it just stops the synchronization. In this case, after unfollowing the main database, you can read and write data in the follower database.

The command expects to be informed of the follower database URL. Here is an example:

```
$ heroku pg:unfollow HEROKU_POSTGRESQL_[COLOR]_URL --app your-app-name
!    HEROKU_POSTGRESQL_[COLOR]_URL will become writable and no longer
!    follow HEROKU_POSTGRESQL_[COLOR]. This cannot be undone.


!    WARNING: Destructive Action
!    This command will affect the app: your-app-name
!    To proceed, type "your-app-name" or re-run this command with
--confirm your-app-name


> your-app-name
Unfollowing HEROKU_POSTGRESQL_[COLOR]_URL... done
```

 An important detail when you perform the unfollow action is that you still continue to be charged by the follower database. This is because the database has not been removed; it still remains active to read and write data.

If you want to delete the database, it is necessary to use the add-on remove command. Here is an example:

```
$ heroku addons:remove HEROKU_POSTGRESQL_[COLOR]_URL --app your-app-name


!    WARNING: Destructive Action
!    This command will affect the app: your-app-name
!    To proceed, type "your-app-name" or re-run this command with
--confirm your-app-name


> your-app-name
Removing HEROKU_POSTGRESQL_[COLOR] on your-app-name... done, v246
   ($200/mo)
```

Upgrade the database plan with follower

A follower database is also an interesting feature to upgrade the database plan with a small amount of downtime.

This operation consists of adding a new follower database with the desired plan and then promoting it to the main database of your application. The advantage of this solution is that the downtime is very low, around 1 minute.

The first step is to create a new follower with the new plan to upgrade:

```
$ heroku addons:add heroku-postgresql:standard-2 --follow DATABASE_URL
--app your-app-name

Adding heroku-postgresql:standard-2 on your-app-name... done, v247 ($200/
mo)

Attached as HEROKU_POSTGRESQL_GOLD_URL

Follower will become available for read-only queries when up-to-date

Use `heroku pg:wait` to track status.

Use `heroku addons:docs heroku-postgresql` to view documentation.
```

The second step is about preventing new updates to the main database so that you can be sure that both databases will be synchronized. This action consists of putting your application in maintenance mode and disabling its processes:

```
$ heroku maintenance:on --app your-app-name

Enabling maintenance mode for your-app-name... done
```

Now, you should also disable your works to prevent any update of data from them:

```
$ heroku ps:scale worker=0 --app your-app-name

Scaling dynos... done, now running worker at 0:2X.
```

After that, you can check whether the follower database is already built through the `heroku pg:wait` command:

```
$ heroku pg:wait --app your-app-name
```

If the command doesn't return anything, it means that the follower database has been created and synchronized with your main database.

Next, you need to promote the follower database to the main database. For this, you first need to perform the unfollow action and after that, promote the database. Through the `heroku pg:info` command, you can see the information on your main database and follower database:

```
$ heroku pg:info --app your-app-name
=== HEROKU_POSTGRESQL_CHARCOAL_URL (DATABASE_URL)
Plan:         Standard Yanari
Status:       Available
...
Followers:    HEROKU_POSTGRESQL_GOLD
...


=== HEROKU_POSTGRESQL_GOLD_URL
Plan:         Standard 2
Status:       Available
...
Following:    HEROKU_POSTGRESQL_CHARCOAL
Behind By:    0 commits
...
```

> The `Behind By` field informs us that the follower database is outdated from the main database by zero commits.

Now, you need to unfollow the main database using the following command:

```
$ heroku pg:unfollow HEROKU_POSTGRESQL_GOLD_URL --app your-app-name
```

The following command promotes it as the main database:

```
$ heroku pg:promote HEROKU_POSTGRESQL_GOLD_URL --app your-app-name
Promoting HEROKU_POSTGRESQL_GOLD_URL to DATABASE_URL... done
```

Finally, activate your works, remove your application from maintenance mode, and delete the old database:

```
$ heroku ps:scale worker=1 --app your-app-name
$ heroku maintenance:off --app your-app-name
$ heroku addons:remove HEROKU_POSTGRESQL_CHARCOAL_URL --app
  your-app-name
```

High availability with followers

By default, the follower databases are created in a geographical area that is different from that of the main database. In addition, all databases in the premium and enterprise plans have high availability enabled. If your database fails, it is automatically replaced by another main database with the same plan. If there are follower databases, they are destroyed and recreated again after the failure event.

Heroku Postgres forking databases

A fork of your database is the structure and data copied at a certain point in time. This consists of creating a new database from another. The fork database is not synchronized after your creation.

The most common use is for analysis and experiments with a copy of the database. You can also use the fork database to experiment with different versions of database plans. This allows you to test the behavior of the database.

A fork database is a copy of another database, that allows us to read and write.

Forking your database

The creation of a fork database works in a manner similar to the creation of a follower database. You must add a new database in the desired plan using the `--fork` flag; this flag advises that there will be a fork from another database.

As it happens with the followers, you don't need to create a fork in the same plan of the database. You can choose any other plan, and the forks allow you to, experiment with different database plans. The forks represent a useful tool to optimize the configuration of your application during these experiments.

The following command illustrates the creation of a new fork database:

```
$ heroku addons:add heroku-postgresql:standard-0 --fork DATABASE_URL
--app your-app-name

Adding heroku-postgresql:standard-0 on your-app-name... done, v249 ($50/
mo)

Attached as HEROKU_POSTGRESQL_ONYX_URL

Database will become available after it completes forking

Use `heroku pg:wait` to track status.

Use `heroku addons:docs heroku-postgresql` to view documentation.
```

Through the `heroku pg:wait` command, you can see the creation of the new database:

```
$ heroku pg:wait --app your-app-name
Waiting for database HEROKU_POSTGRESQL_ONYX_URL... / preparing
  (5% completed)
```

Forking databases with the fast option

There is another option to create a fork database, and it is through the use of the `--fast` flag. This mode of creation is faster because the fork is made 30 hours ago; this is the maximum period. It could be a useful option if your database doesn't have big changes over this period. This option is presented here as an alternative if you need to create a fork quickly:

```
$ heroku addons:add heroku-postgresql:standard-2 --fork DATABASE_URL
--fast --app your-app-name
Adding heroku-postgresql:standard-2 on your-app-name... done, v250 ($200/
mo)
Attached as HEROKU_POSTGRESQL_ROSE_URL
Fork will contain data from October 14, 2014  3:10PM UTC (about 22 hours
ago)
To create a fork with up-to-date data, exclude the `--fast` flag.
Database will become available after it completes forking
Use `heroku pg:wait` to track status.
Use `heroku addons:docs heroku-postgresql` to view documentation.
```

View your fork databases

You can use the `heroku pg:info` command to view information on your fork database:

```
$ heroku pg:info --app your-app-name
=== HEROKU_POSTGRESQL_ROSE_URL
Plan:        Standard 2
Status:      Available
Data Size:   56.0 MB
Tables:      38
PG Version:  9.3.5
Connections: 1/400
```

```
Fork/Follow:  Available
Rollback:     earliest from 2014-10-15 13:15 UTC
Created:      2014-10-15 13:10 UTC
Forked From:  HEROKU_POSTGRESQL_CHARCOAL
Maintenance:  not required
```

Deprovisioning a fork database

You can remove a fork database at any time. This action deletes the database via the `heroku addons:remove` command using the database color URL as a parameter:

```
$ heroku addons:remove HEROKU_POSTGRESQL_[COLOR]_URL --app
  your-app-name
!     WARNING: Destructive Action
!     This command will affect the app: rsvp-production
!     To proceed, type "your-app-name" or re-run this command with
--confirm your-app-name


> your-app-name
Removing HEROKU_POSTGRESQL_[COLOR] on your-app-name... done, v251
  ($200/mo)
```

Self-test questions

Answer true or false.

1. Is rollback a feature that allows you to create a database in the previous state in time?

2. Is the --by flag mandatory to create a rollback database?

3. After creating a rollback database, is it necessary to promote a main database to active it in your application?

4. Is a follower database an important resource for the horizontal growth of your database as a master and slave?

5. Are follower databases synchronized automatically?

6. Can follower databases be created with different database plans?

7. Are fork databases an interesting resource for experiments with a copy of the main database?

8. Do fork databases allow us to create a new follower and fork database with your content?

9. Is a fork database a database that is constantly synchronized with the main database?

10. Is heroku pg:wait a useful command to monitor the creation of new databases?

Summary

In this chapter, you learned important concepts and tools that you will probably use as your applications grow.

First, you saw the Heroku Postgres rollback. This is very useful when data loss occurs accidentally. With one command, you can create a new database with the old state of your main database.

You learned about working with follower databases. The followers probably will be one of the features that you will use as your application grows up. Through followers, Heroku created a master-slave solution for database reading.

Finally, you learned about fork databases. A fork is a copy of the database, and it isn't synchronized with the main database. You also learned that forks are interesting to experiment and test with different database plans.

In the next chapter, you will learn how logs work and how to extract information that helps you identify problems and understand the most common errors.

7

Understanding
Log Statements and
Common Errors

Logs are important tools to discover problems and failures in your applications. Through logs, it is possible to identify the causes and find appropriate solutions. Heroku Postgres provides all logs generated by your databases.

The main component in the Heroku structure is the Logplex. It collects logs from different sources and provides them in a single channel so that you can analyze them and take appropriate actions in real time.

In this chapter, you will learn how to view logs. You will understand the most common errors and also learn how to collect metrics from the logs.

This chapter will cover:

- Log statements
- Common errors
- Metrics logs

Log statements

The first step is to ensure that you have access to all logs in real time. The Heroku client provides the `heroku logs` command that allows you to view all logs collected by the Logplex in a unified manner. Using this command, you can filter through the postgres process to view only database logs. You can also use the `-t` option (tail); this opens a continuous stream of data logs. Here is an example:

```
$ heroku logs -p postgres -t --app your-app-name
2014-11-01T23:41:42Z app[postgres.10]: [CHARCOAL] checkpoint
   complete: wrote 0 buffers (0.0%); 0 transaction log file(s) added,
      0 removed, 1 recycled; write=0.000 s, sync=0.000 s,
         total=0.004 s; sync files=0, longest=0.000 s, average=0.000 s
```

This way, you can view the logs generated by your Postgres database, perform the diagnosis, and identify the common errors.

The heroku logs command provides the following options to display the recent log output:

- `-n, --num NUM`: This refers to the number of lines to display
- `-p, --ps PS`: This only display logs from the given process
- `-s, --source SOURCE`: This only display logs from the given source
- `-t, --tail`: This refers to continually streaming logs

 The logs are available for production database plans. They are not available for plans in the Hobby tier.

Common errors

There are a number of common errors that can be easily identified through the logs. Understanding these errors and analyzing can help you in the process of continuous database improvement.

Then you will understand the most common ones so that you can take the necessary action in order to solve them.

LOG: long duration

Queries that take longer than 2 seconds are logged automatically so that you can identify and optimize your code. These logs are generated in the following format:

```
[8-2] g0afa5bjht [GOLD] LOG: duration: 63.697 ms statement:
  SELECT "courses".* FROM "courses"...
```

If there are large numbers of these logs, probably your application has performance problems. A good recommendation is to try to reduce the execution time of your queries by 10 ms. You can achieve this optimization by adding indexes or using the EXPLAIN command from PostgreSQL to understand the performance issues in your query.

LOG: unexpected EOF on client connection

This error occurs when your application does not disconnect the Postgres database appropriately. It indicates that there was a connection loss between the application and the database; this states that the connection was not clear and the problem still remains. The following example illustrates this situation:

```
app[postgres]: LOG: could not receive data from client: Connection reset
by peer app[postgres]: LOG: unexpected EOF on client connection

heroku[router]: at=error code=H13 desc="Connection closed without
response" method=GET path=/crash host=alphabeta.herokuapp.com dyno=web.1
connect=1ms service=10ms status=503 bytes=0

heroku[web.1]: Process exited with status 1

heroku[web.1]: State changed from up to crashed
```

The recommended solution for this problem is to analyze the logs relating to your application and identify the causes of this connection loss. Usually, this error is related to the code that implements the database connection.

PGError: permission denied for relation

This error occurs when you are working with the database plan in the Hobby tier. It has limitations on the amount of records that can be inserted into the database. When this limit is reached, the following log line appears:

```
PGError: ERROR:  permission denied for relation courses
```

In order to solve this problem, you should migrate to another database plan in the production tier that does not provide constraints on the amount of records.

PGError: operator does not exist

You may see this error when different data types are compared without performing the casting, for example, a string comparison with an integer. A log similar to the following one will appear:

```
PGError: ERROR:  operator does not exist: character varying = integer
```

The solution for this error is to fix the SQL so that it uses the appropriate casting or change the SQL query for the same data type.

PGError: relation "table-name" does not exist

This is a standard error when you try to access a table in the database that does not exist:

```
PGError: ERROR: relation "students" does not exist
```

You can solve this problem by checking whether all database migrations were performed or by checking whether your SQL syntax is written correctly.

PGError: column "column-name" cannot...

This is an error that occurs when PostgreSQL does not know how to convert the data type to another format. For example, if you have a string out of the pattern and the database attempts to transform it into a date, the following log is generated:

```
PGError: ERROR: column "created_at" cannot be cast to type "date"
```

You can solve this error by fixing the problem in the column data or checking whether your SQL query is written correctly.

PGError: SSL SYSCALL error: EOF detected

This is an error that indicates a problem on the client side. It can occur because of two situations: the first is a sharing connection problem between more than one process, and the second one is due to an abrupt disconnection on the client side:

```
PGError: ERROR: SSL SYSCALL error: EOF detected:
  SELECT "doctors".* FROM "doctors" ORDER BY id DESC LIMIT 10
```

This error is commonly solved by Heroku. It automatically detects the problem, kills the dyno, and creates a new dyno, thus re-establishing the connection.

PGError: prepared statement "a30" already exists

This is another problem related to sharing a connection between multiple processes when the client side tries to prepare a statement with a name already used by another process, usually without clearing the original statement.

To solve this problem, you need to consider all current processes and make the necessary corrections to avoid the sharing connection problem.

FATAL: too many connections for role

You may find this error when you are using the plans in the Hobby tier. They offer a limitation of 20 simultaneous connections to the database, thus displaying this log message:

```
FATAL:  too many connections for role "[role name]"
```

There are several suggestions to solve this problem. The first one is to close some connections with the database that you are not using, and the other suggestion is to migrate the database plan for one that supports a larger number of connections.

FATAL: could not receive data...

This problem is associated with database replication to a follower database when a network problem or a SSL failed negotiation occurs. The following error is logged:

```
FATAL: could not receive data from WAL stream: SSL error: sslv3 alert
  unexpected message
```

The solution to this problem is executed automatically by the Heroku architecture, so the network problem or SSL is resolved. The primary database completes the synchronization with the follower database.

FATAL: role "role-name"...

This is an error that occurs when the database is deprovisioned but its connection still exists:

```
FATAL: role "g5hja7jkeu" is not permitted to log in (PG::Error)
```

There are two solutions for this problem: the first one is to provision a new database through the `heroku adds:add heroku-postgresql` command, and the second one is to promote one database as a primary database through the `heroku pg:promote HEROKU_POSTGRESQL_[COLOR]_URL` command.

FATAL: terminating connection due to administrator command

This error is caused when the connection process with the database is killed. This can be accomplished in two ways: through the `heroku pg:kill` command and by running the `SELECT pg_cancel_backend(pid)` query. The following log is generated:

```
FATAL: terminating connection due to administrator command
```

FATAL: remaining connection slots are reserved for non-replication superuser connections

All database plans on Heroku Postgres have a maximum number of connections; this error is generated when the number of connections has been reached. Also, it indicates that there are a number of connections reserved for the Heroku team:

```
FATAL: remaining connection slots are reserved for non-replication
    superuser connections
```

The indicated solution for this problem is to search for idle connections and kill their processes. Another suggestion is to migrate to a database plan that supports a higher number of connections.

Temporary file: path "file path", size "file size"

This is an informational log; it announces that the maximum size for temporary logs, which is 10240 KB, has been reached. These logs are used for temporary queries. Overuse of these temporary logs can impact SQL query performance:

```
temporary file: path "base/pgsql_tmp/pgsql_tmp234678.434", size
    1075741736
```

Metrics logs

Heroku Postgres has a log statement that provides metrics on database usage. This feature is important to monitor the behavior of the database over time.

The metrics information helps you improve database configurations, and identify critical issues, it also teaches you how to improve your application's architecture.

To view the metrics logs, you should use the `heroku logs` command by filtering through the `heroku-postgres` process, as shown in the following example:

```
$ heroku logs -p heroku-postgres -t --app your-app-name
2014-11-02T00:35:38+00:00 app[heroku-postgres]: source=HEROKU_POSTGRESQL_
CHARCOAL sample#current_transaction=179097 sample#db_size=61229240bytes
sample#tables=38 sample#active-connections=9 sample#waiting-connections=0
sample#index-cache-hit-rate=0.99999 sample#table-cache-hit-rate=1
sample#load-avg-1m=0.395 sample#load-avg-5m=0.44 sample#load-avg-
15m=0.435 sample#read-iops=17.042 sample#write-iops=1.7437 sample#memory-
total=7629452kB sample#memory-free=64876kB sample#memory-cached=6838076kB
sample#memory-postgres=364248kB
```

 The information on the metrics is available in the standard, premium, and enterprise plans.

The following list will help you understand every piece of information available for each attribute.

- The logs show the timestamp of the period measurement.

- **source**: This is the database associated with data measurement.

- **sample#db_size**: The byte number contained in the database. This includes all tables and indexes, including the database bloat data.

- **sample#tables**: The table numbers in the database.

- **sample#active-connections**: The connection numbers established in the database.

- **sample#current_transaction**: The current transaction ID.

- **sample#index-cache-hit-rate**: The rate of the lookups index provided by the shared buffer cache, rounded to 5 decimal points.

- **sample#table-cache-hit-rate**: The rate of table lookups provided by the shared buffer cache, rounded to 5 decimal points.

- **sample#waiting-connections**: Connection numbers waiting to be purchased. If many connections are waiting, this can be a sign of database concurrence mistreated.

- **sample#load-avg-1m, sample#load-avg-5m** and **sample#load-avg-15m**: The system load average within 1 minute, 5 minutes, and 15 minutes, divided by the number of available CPUs.

- **sample#read-iops** and **sample#writes-iops**: The number of reads and writes for each block of 16 KB of I/O.

- **sample#memory-total**: Total available memory in KB.

- **sample#memory-free**: Total free memory in KB.

- **sample#memory-cached**: Total cache memory in KB.

- **sample#memory-postgres**: Approximate total of memory used by PostgreSQL in KB.

Self-test questions

Answer true or false.

1. Are logs important information source for identifying problems in your database?

2. Does the heroku logs command only show database logs?

3. Is the Postgres process necessary to filter the database logs?

4. Is Logplex a feature that allows a unified view of logs?

5. Can errors be divided into three common categories: LOG, FATAL, and PGError?

6. Is there an error that informs users if the query is taking more than 2 seconds?

7. Do the plans in the Hobby tier offer many limitations?

8. Should you always be careful about processes that use the same connection with the database?

9. Can you view important information about database metrics through the `heroku logs` command using the `heroku-postgres` filter?

10. Is the metrics data log with sample# information just examples?

Summary

In this chapter, you learned how to access logs generated by Heroku Postgres. You understood that logs are important tools for investigating and solving problems related to your application and database. You also learned how to identify and solve the most common errors that may occur.

In the last part of this chapter, you learned how to gather metrics information on your database. You understood that this information is important for you to make decisions in order to improve your database, and that some issues can be resolved by optimizing your application.

In the next and final chapter of this book, you will learn about some additional issues necessary for many developers, and you will learn how to use some tools such as full text search, data caching, PostGIS, and some other interesting extensions.

8

Extensions, PostGIS, Full Text Search Dictionaries, Data Caching, and Tuning

In the previous chapters, you've learned the main concepts about Heroku Postgres, which usually cover most of the functions that you will need.

You have reached the last chapter and this is a very special chapter because it covers a collection of advanced features that I preferred to cover just in one chapter as an excellent reference for you.

In this chapter, you will learn about the main extensions of the Postgres database, and understand how to enable PostGIS to work with spatial data, text search tools, and data cache. You will also gauge how you can perform optimizations and performance analysis in your database.

This chapter covers the following topics:

- Heroku Postgres extensions
- Full text search dictionaries
- Data caching
- Setting up PostGIS
- Database tuning
- Performance analysis

Heroku Postgres extensions

PostgreSQL allows its functionality to be extended with additional modules called extensions. Many of these extensions aren't installed by default in PostgreSQL, because they aren't part of its core and mainly because they are specific to a limited audience. In addition, some extensions are experimental, but nothing prevents their use.

Heroku Postgres provides some interesting extensions for data types, functions, statistics, index types, languages, searches, and many others. In the next sections, you will learn about each of these extensions, with simple samples, and you will understand how they work.

The first step to get started is to discover the list of available extensions in your database; it may vary according your database plan. You should do it using the following command:

```
$ echo 'show extwlist.extensions' | heroku pg:psql --app your-app-name
---> Connecting to HEROKU_POSTGRESQL_CHARCOAL_URL (DATABASE_URL)
extwlist.extensions
-----------------------------------------------------------------btr
ee_gist,chkpass,citext,cube,dblink,dict_int,dict_xsyn,
earthdistance,fuzzystrmatch,hstore,isn,ltree,pg_stat_statements,
pg_trgm,pgcrypto,pgrowlocks,pgstattuple,plpgsql,plv8,postgis,
postgis_topology,postgres_fdw,tablefunc,unaccent,uuid-ossp
```

These extensions are available in the database, but they aren't installed. To install and start using its features, you need to run the appropriate SQL query in the database. First you need to connect in `psql` and then run the SQL query to install the extension that you want:

```
$ heroku pg:psql --app your-app-name
---> Connecting to HEROKU_POSTGRESQL_GOLD_URL (DATABASE_URL)
psql (9.3.4, server 9.3.3)
SSL connection (cipher: DHE-RSA-AES256-SHA, bits: 256)
Type "help" for help.
app-name::GOLD=> CREATE EXTENSION extension_name_to_install;
```

Data types

In computer science, data type is a combination of values and operations that one variable can perform. There are a large number of data types available such as integer, float, Boolean, Array, Hash, and many others. PostgreSQL is no different; you have a collection of data types available by default, such as numeric, monetary, character, binary, date/time, Boolean, enumerated, and many others.

In some cases, other kinds of data types are necessary and they aren't installed by default on PostgreSQL. In this section, you will discover the power of some important extensions for data types.

Case-insensitive text – citext

This data type is very useful for working with queries where the data is case insensitive. You can use this feature with an implementation to facilitate your searches, such as searching for products on an e-commerce website.

For you to understand, the data type text is generally used, but it is case sensitive. For example, suppose you have a table with the column username and an index to avoid duplicate usernames:

```
$ heroku pg:psql -app your-app-name
CREATE TABLE students (username text NOT NULL);
CREATE UNIQUE INDEX unique_username_on_students ON students
  (username);
```

Next, you'll insert some student names:

```
INSERT INTO students (username) VALUES ('patrick');
INSERT INTO students (username) VALUES ('PATRICK');
```

In the preceding example, two records were created; as the data type text is case sensitive, so the values 'patrick' and 'PATRICK' are different. This is the problem that extension citext resolves, it allows you to define case insensitive data.

After that, you'll switch to use the citext extension:

```
CREATE EXTENSION citext;
TRUNCATE TABLE students;
ALTER TABLE students ALTER COLUMN username TYPE citext;
DROP INDEX unique_username_on_students;
CREATE UNIQUE INDEX unique_username_on_students ON students
  (username);
```

Finally, if you try to repeat the inserts, you'll have an error:

```
INSERT INTO students (username) VALUES ('patrick');
INSERT INTO students (username) VALUES ('PATRICK');
# ERROR: duplicate key value violates unique constraint
  "unique_username_on_students"
# DETAIL: Key (username)=(PATRICK) already exists.
```

You can find more information at `http://www.postgresql.org/docs/current/static/citext.html`.

Cube

The `cube` extension is used to create multidimensional data. It is useful for datasets that require more than one dimension. Through this extension, you can perform many operations with multidimensional data such as discovering the number of dimensions, creating union between cubes, finding the intersection of two cubes, generating subsets, and other functions. In the following example, you will see how to create a cube and how to perform some queries.

```
$ heroku pg:psql --app your-app-name
CREATE EXTENSION cube;
CREATE TABLE sets (element cube);
INSERT INTO sets (element) VALUES ('(1, 2, 3)');
```

First, you'll check whether the cube contains a specific subset:

```
SELECT * FROM sets WHERE cube_contains(element, '(1, 2)');
   element
-----------
 (1, 2, 3)
```

After that, you'll create a cube union with another cube:

```
SELECT cube_union(element, '(4, 5, 6)') FROM sets;
      cube_union
---------------------
 (1, 2, 3),(4, 5, 6)
```

Finally, you will find the cube intersection with another cube:

```
SELECT cube_inter(element, '(1, 2)') FROM sets;

     cube_inter

--------------------

 (1, 2, 3),(1, 2, 0)
```

There are other functions that you can explore. For more information, visit the website http://www.postgresql.org/docs/current/static/cube.html.

HStore

The HStore extension stores data in key and value format. It is a data structure consisting of a non-ordered set of items formed by a key-value pair, in which each key has an associated value. The HStore data type is useful because it allows their use in queries.

In the following example, you will create a new table called profiles and store a data key / value in the configs column.

```
$ heroku pg:psql --app your-app-name

CREATE EXTENSION hstore;

CREATE TABLE profiles (configs hstore);

INSERT INTO profiles (configs) VALUES ('resolution => "1024x768",
   brightness => 45');
```

This data type has a limitation where all their data is stored in string format. You can see that if you perform a SELECT query:

```
SELECT * FROM profiles;
                     configs

----------------------------------------------

 "brightness"=>"45", "resolution"=>"1024x768"
```

Finally, you are able to find records using the configs key-value data:

```
SELECT * FROM profiles WHERE configs->'resolution' = '1024x768';
                     configs

----------------------------------------------

 "brightness"=>"45", "resolution"=>"1024x768"
```

There are numerous possibilities of using the `HStore` extension and you can find more information in the PostgreSQL documentation `http://www.postgresql.org/docs/current/static/hstore.html`.

Label tree – ltree

It provides a way to organize data with labels stored in a hierarchical tree structure. The main advantage of this extension is the speed for searching data, since a recursive search is not necessary.

For you to understand this extension better, you can build an example of continents and countries in a hierarchical tree as shown in the following diagram:

Hierarchical tree of countries.

First, you will install the `ltree` extension, then create the table of countries and add the tree structure as shown in the preceding diagram. The commands for creating the country table are as follows:

```
$ heroku pg:psql --app your-app-name
CREATE EXTENSION ltree;
CREATE TABLE countries (path ltree);
INSERT INTO countries VALUES ('Earth');
INSERT INTO countries VALUES ('Earth.Africa');
INSERT INTO countries VALUES ('Earth.Africa.Nigeria');
INSERT INTO countries VALUES ('Earth.Africa.Angola');
INSERT INTO countries VALUES ('Earth.Europe');
INSERT INTO countries VALUES ('Earth.Europe.France');
INSERT INTO countries VALUES ('Earth.Asia');
INSERT INTO countries VALUES ('Earth.Asia.Japan');
INSERT INTO countries VALUES ('Earth.Asia.China');
```

Finally, you are able to perform queries to discover the countries on each continent. For example if you want to view countries of Africa use the following query:

```
SELECT path FROM countries WHERE path ~ 'Earth.Africa.*{1}';
        path
- - - - - - - - - - - - - - - - - - - -
 Earth.Africa.Nigeria
 Earth.Africa.Angola
```

If you want to view countries in Europe use the following query:

```
SELECT path FROM countries WHERE path ~ 'Earth.Europe.*{1}';
        path
- - - - - - - - - - - - - - - - - - - -
 Earth.Europe.France
```

If you want to view countries in Asia use the following query:

```
SELECT path FROM countries WHERE path ~ 'Earth.Asia.*{1}';
        path
- - - - - - - - - - - - - - - -
 Earth.Asia.Japan
 Earth.Asia.China
```

This extension can be used in many situations, and has many functions for searching. You can find more information in its documentation at http://www.postgresql. org/docs/current/static/ltree.html.

Product numbering – isn

Data types are used to store product data following the international standard and serial numbers such as ISSN (serial), UPC, ISBN (books), EAN13, ISMN (music). The numbers are validated.

In this example, you will create a table of books, with the data type ISBN for the id field, and you will insert a book:

```
$ heroku pg:psql --app your-app-name
CREATE EXTENSION isn;
CREATE TABLE books (id isbn, name text);
INSERT INTO books (id, name) VALUES ('9780307465351', 'The 4-Hour
  Workweek');
```

This extension is very simple and you can find all data types supported in the documentation at `http://www.postgresql.org/docs/current/static/isn.html`.

Functions

In computer science, functions are subprograms identified by a name. They can receive a list of parameters and one of the great benefits is the reuse of code. In addition, they make the code reading more intuitive.

All the function extensions on PostgreSQL provide a set of methods that increase the power and features of your database. They provide algorithms to solve common problems. In the upcoming sections, you will learn the available function extensions in Heroku Postgres.

Earth distance

The `earthdistance` extension offers two different ways to calculate distances in a circle on the earth's surface. For this extension, the earth is assumed to be perfectly spherical. If the calculations are inaccurate for you, it's recommended to use the `PostGIS` extension. You will see more about it in this chapter.

In this example, you will create a table of attractions in Brazil and you will insert their latitude/longitude. After using this information, you will find the distance between the two attractions. You can create the following table:

```
id  |              name             |  latitude  |  longitude
----+-------------------------------+------------+-----------
 1  | Christ the Redeemer (statue)  | -22.9518769 | -43.2104991
 2  | Maracana Stadium              | -22.9121089 | -43.2301558
```

First, you will install the `earthdistance` extension and then insert the two attractions:

```
$ heroku pg:psql --app your-app-name
CREATE EXTENSION earthdistance;
CREATE TABLE attractions (id integer, name text, latitude float,
  longitude float);
INSERT INTO attractions (id, name, latitude, longitude) VALUES
  (1, 'Christ the Redeemer (statue)', -22.951876900000000000,
   -43.210499099999990000);
INSERT INTO attractions (id, name, latitude, longitude) VALUES
  (2, 'Maracana Stadium', -22.912108900000000000,
   -43.230155800000034000);
```

Finally, you are able to calculate the distance between the `Christ the Redeemer (statue)` and `Maracana Stadium`. In this example, you will use two functions, the first one is the `ll_to_earth` function, which transforms the latitude/longitude data on a point on the surface of the Earth. The second function is `earth_distance` that calculates the distance.

```
SELECT earth_distance(
    (SELECT ll_to_earth(latitude, longitude) FROM attractions WHERE name =
'Christ the Redeemer (statue)'),
    (SELECT ll_to_earth(latitude, longitude) FROM attractions WHERE name =
'Maracana Stadium')
);
  earth_distance
------------------
 4864.08588226038
```

There are other possibilities for this extension; visit the documentation at http://www.postgresql.org/docs/current/static/earthdistance.html.

Intarray

This extension provides a set of functions and operators for working with integer arrays. It also provides support for indexed search using operators. The operations provided by this extension are used for one-dimensional arrays.

In this example, you will create a table of contents and add a disordered array. Then you will use two functions, the first to sort the array and the second to display the number of elements.

To start, you will install the `intarray` extension, create the table contents, and insert a record:

```
$ heroku pg:psql --app your-app-name
CREATE EXTENSION intarray;
CREATE TABLE contents (elements INT[]);
INSERT INTO contents (elements) VALUES (ARRAY[2, 4, 3, 1]);
```

Next, you will sort the array of elements:

```
SELECT sort_asc(elements) FROM contents;
sort_asc
-----------
 {1,2,3,4}
```

Finally, you will discover the number of elements in the array.

```
SELECT icount(elements) FROM contents;
icount

--------

        4
```

For other useful functions, check the documentation at http://www.postgresql.org/docs/current/static/intarray.html.

Fuzzy match – fuzzystrmatch

This extension provides a set of functions for determining the distance and similarity between strings. Search engines such as Google search for similar words; through the extension fuzzystrmatch you are able to use this feature in your queries.

In the following example, you will add some names and use the function called difference to discover their similarity. This function returns a value from 0 to 4, where 0 (zero) is the exact match and 4 (four) is the distant correspondence:

```
$ heroku pg:psql --app your-app-name
CREATE EXTENSION fuzzystrmatch;
CREATE TABLE doctors (name text);
INSERT INTO doctors (name) VALUES ('Patrick');
INSERT INTO doctors (name) VALUES ('Padrig');
SELECT difference(
    (SELECT name FROM doctors WHERE name = 'Patrick'),
    (SELECT name FROM doctors WHERE name = 'Padrig')
);
difference

------------

        4
```

There are other functions such as soundex, levenshtein, metaphone, and dmetaphone. You can find more information about them on the extension documentation at http://www.postgresql.org/docs/current/static/fuzzystrmatch.html.

PGCrypto

This extension provides encryption functions that allow you to store encrypted data in your database. The pgcrypto extension is often used to manage user authentication in web applications.

In the following example, you will create a user table with two columns: username and password. Now you will insert a user with an encrypted password. Then, through the appropriate SQL, you will search the user with the access credentials.

```
$ heroku pg:psql --app your-app-name
CREATE EXTENSION pgcrypto;
CREATE TABLE users (username text, password bytea);
```

In the following insert statement, you will encrypt the user password via the digest function. This function accepts two parameters: the first one is the string to be encrypted and the second one is the type of algorithm that is used. The algorithm can be md5, sha1, sha224, sha256, sha384, or sha512.

```
INSERT INTO users (username, password) VALUES ('patrickespake',
  digest('pass123', 'md5'));
```

Finally, you are able to search users via the username and password.

```
SELECT * FROM users WHERE username = 'patrickespake' AND
  password = digest('pass123', 'md5') LIMIT 1;
    username     |                   password
----------------+-------------------------------------------
 patrickespake  | 2%\001p\240\334\251-S\354\226$\3636\312$
```

In the documentation at http://www.postgresql.org/docs/current/static/pgcrypto.html, you can find many other interesting functions.

Table functions and pivot tables – tablefunc

This is an extension that allows you to return tables with multiple lines. It provides useful functions for working with pivot tables. It is used to cross-refer values of two variables.

In the following example, you will create a sales table with the columns year, month, and value. Then you will use this data to make a crosstab by monthly sales.

First, you will install the `tablefunc` extension and insert some sales:

```
$ heroku pg:psql --app your-app-name
CREATE EXTENSION tablefunc;
CREATE TABLE sales (year integer, month integer, value float);
INSERT INTO sales (year, month, value) VALUES (2013, 1, 34.56);
INSERT INTO sales (year, month, value) VALUES (2014, 3, 99.50);
INSERT INTO sales (year, month, value) VALUES (2014, 4, 45.99);
INSERT INTO sales (year, month, value) VALUES (2015, 2, 78.99);
```

Finally, you will use the functions `crosstab` and `generate_series` to create a pivot table between month and the sales value in each year:

```
SELECT * FROM crosstab(
    'SELECT year, month, value FROM sales',
    'SELECT month FROM generate_series(1, 4) month'
  )
  AS (
    year integer,
    "Jan" float,
    "Feb" float,
    "Mar" float,
    "Apr" float
  );
```

year	Jan	Feb	Mar	Apr
2013	34.56			
2014			99.5	45.99
2015		78.99		

For more information visit the documentation at `http://www.postgresql.org/docs/current/static/tablefunc.html`.

Trigram – pg_trgm

The `pg_trgm` extension provides operators and functions to calculate the similarity of alphanumeric ASCII text with a trigram base match. A trigram is defined with a set of three consecutive characters, made from a string; it is very effective for measuring the similarity of words in natural languages.

The following example is very simple; you will use the `similarity` function to discover the similarity between two strings. The return of this function can be between 0 and 1, where 0 (zero) indicates that the strings are dissimilar and 1 (one) being similar.

```
$ heroku pg:psql --app your-app-name
CREATE EXTENSION pg_trgm;
SELECT similarity('PostgreSQL', 'Postgres');
similarity
------------
   0.666667
```

You can find more information at http://www.postgresql.org/docs/current/static/pgtrgm.html.

UUID generation

It provides functions to generate universal unique identifiers (UUID). It is a special type of identifier used in software applications to provide a reference number that is unique in any context.

```
$ heroku pg:psql --app your-app-name
CREATE EXTENSION "uuid-ossp";
SELECT uuid_generate_v1();
         uuid_generate_v1
--------------------------------------
 d976c6de-af2e-11e4-b1fb-22000ae18ca6
```

For more information, visit the documentation at http://www.postgresql.org/docs/current/static/uuid-ossp.html.

Statistics

By definition, statistics is the science that uses probabilistic theories to explain the frequency of the occurrence of events. The Heroku Postgres provides some extensions for database statistics and tables. In upcoming sections, you will learn about them.

Row locking – pgrowlocks

This extension provides a function called `pgrowlocks` to display locked rows in a specific table.

First, you must install the extension:

```
$ heroku pg:psql --app your-app-name
CREATE EXTENSION pgrowlocks;
```

The `pgrowlocks` function accepts a parameter that is the table name. For example:

```
SELECT * FROM pgrowlocks('users');
```

locked_row	lock_type	locker	multi	xids	pids
(0,1)	Shared	22	t	{378,809}	{23457}
(0,2)	Exclusive	345	f	{780}	{12869}

For details, visit the documentation at `http://www.postgresql.org/docs/current/static/pgrowlocks.html`.

Tuple statistics – pgstattuple

A tuple is a set of objects that share the same characteristics or have the same property. The `pgstattuple` extension provides a set of functions for statistics on the tuple level.

In the official Heroku documentation, it is informed that this extension is available for use, but many developers fail to use it. This extension needs a superuser level and Heroku does not provide it. For example:

```
$ heroku pg:psql --app your-app-name
CREATE EXTENSION pgstattuple;
CREATE TABLE jobs (id integer, name text);
INSERT INTO jobs (id, name) VALUES (1, 'Load users');
INSERT INTO jobs (id, name) VALUES (2, 'Send emails');
SELECT * FROM pgstattuple('jobs');
ERROR:  must be superuser to use pgstattuple functions
```

You can find more information about using this extension in your local environment at `http://www.postgresql.org/docs/current/static/pgstattuple.html`.

Index types

An index, in the database context, is a related reference to a key, which is used for optimization purposes and and to allow records to be located more rapidly in a query. Heroku Postgres provides an extension to work with index types `Btree GiST`.

Btree GiST – btree_gist

In computing, **Generalized Search Tree (GiST)** is a data structure that can be used to build search tree in many types of data. The `btree_gist` extension provides the GiST index operator that implements the equivalent B-tree behavior for these data types: `int2`, `int4`, `int8`, `float4`, `float8`, `numeric`, `timestamp`, `time`, `date`, `interval`, `oid`, `money`, `char`, `varchar`, `text`, `bytea`, `bit`, `varbit`, `macaddr`, `inet`, and `cidr`.

Most of the time, these operator classes will not exceed B-tree index methods and don't have the ability to enforce uniqueness.

These operator classes are useful when a multicolumn GiST index is required.

For example:

```
$ heroku pg:psql --app your-app-name
CREATE EXTENSION btree_gist;
CREATE TABLE drinks (quantity int4);
CREATE INDEX drinks_quantity_index ON drinks USING gist (quantity);
```

For more details visit the documentation at `http://www.postgresql.org/docs/current/static/btree-gist.html`.

Languages

PostgreSQL allows user-defined functions. They are written in other programming languages. These languages are generically called **procedural languages (PLs)**. Heroku only supports one extra extension: PLV8.

PLV8 – V8 Engine JavaScript Procedural Language

This extension is very interesting because it provides a procedural language created by the JavaScript V8 engine. It allows you to write functions in JavaScript and use them with SQL.

In the following example, you will create a function in JavaScript that makes a join between two JSON objects.

First, you will install the PLV8 extension and then the `join_json` function. This function accepts two JSON objects as parameters:

```
$ heroku pg:psql --app your-app-name
CREATE EXTENSION plv8;
CREATE OR REPLACE FUNCTION join_json(first JSON, second JSON)
RETURNS JSON AS $$
  for (var json_key in second)
  {
    first[json_key] = second[json_key];
  }
  return first;
$$ LANGUAGE plv8;
```

Finally, you will run SQL to make a union between the two JSON objects.

```
WITH my_join AS (
  SELECT
    '{"config":"true"}'::JSON f,
    '{"user":23}'::JSON s
)
SELECT
  f,
  s,
  join_json(f, s)
FROM my_join;
          f        |      s      |              join_json
------------------+-------------+----------------------------
{"config":"true"}|{"user":23}|{"config":"true","user":23}
```

The PLV8 extension is not available on the Hobby-tier database plans.

For more information visit the project page at `https://code.google.com/p/plv8js/`.

Full text search dictionaries

Full text search dictionaries are a mechanism that allows the identification of documents in natural language corresponding to a query and optionally sorts them by relevance. In the upcoming sections, you will use two of these extensions.

Dict int

This is a full-text search dictionary extension used for indexing integers (signed and unsigned), preventing the growth of the unique word number, which greatly affects the search performance.

```
$ heroku pg:psql --app your-app-name
CREATE EXTENSION dict_int;
```

For more details, visit the documentation at `http://www.postgresql.org/docs/current/static/dict-int.html`.

Unaccent

Basically, this consists of a text searching and filtering dictionary, which means that its output is always passed to the next dictionary, which is different from the normal behavior of dictionaries. This extension removes accents from lexemes. It is the minimum unit of distinctive semantic system of a language.

```
$ heroku pg:psql --app your-app-name
CREATE EXTENSION unaccent;
```

For more details, visit the documentation at `http://www.postgresql.org/docs/current/static/unaccent.html`.

Data caching

Generally, for most applications, only one piece of data is frequently accessed. Postgres monitors the accessed data and places it in a cache to improve the performance of your queries. If your application is well designed, it is possible that 99 percent of the queries are cached.

You can find the cache rate of your database with the following SQL query:

```
$ heroku pg:psql --app your-app-name
SELECT sum(heap_blks_hit) / (sum(heap_blks_hit) + sum(heap_blks_read)) as
percentage, sum(heap_blks_hit) as quantity_hit, sum(heap_blks_read) as
quantity_read FROM pg_statio_user_tables;
      percentage      |  quantity_hit   | quantity_read
----------------------+-----------------+---------------
 0.99999826000612665185 |    4024719812   |       7003
(1 row)
```

In this example, the application and the database are optimized with 99.99 percent of cache. If your percentage is below that, you should consider optimizing your application or change your database plan to a higher one that offers more RAM memory.

For example, if you are using the Premium 2 plan that offers 3.5 GB of RAM memory, a small portion will be used by the operating system kernel, another part will be used for other programs, including Postgres, and the rest between 80 percent and 95 percent of RAM memory is used to cache data by the operating system. Postgres manages a Shared Buffer Cache, which is allocated and used to hold data and indexes in memory. Usually, it is allocated 25 percent of the total operating system memory.

Some operations in the database can affect the amount of cache memory temporarily. If, for example, you are running VACUUM, DDL operations, or creating indexes, these operations tend to consume the available cache memory.

If there is an interruption of database services, you may receive a message saying that you have a "cold cache". This happens for a period until the database comes back online after a service failure.

As a result, it will drop the quality of your application during cache recreation. One way to solve this is using a follower of your primary database so that, when the failure occurs, you can promote the follower database as the main database and reduce the time for the cache. This way you can ensure greater stability in failure events.

Setting up PostGIS

PostGIS is an extension for creating spatial databases in PostgreSQL. This extension adds support for geographic objects; it allows location queries through SQL.

This is the most popular open source extension offering many features that are rarely found in competing spatial databases such as Oracle Locator/Spatial and SQL Server.

PostGIS is supported on Heroku Postgres in beta mode. For using this extension, you must be using a database in the production tier and it isn't available for plans in the Hobby tier. Besides that, it is only available in the 2.0 version with Postgres v9.2 or in the 2.1 version with Postgres v9.3.

Provisioning

You can install PostGIS as any other extension. First you must connect to `psql` and then run the statement for installation:

```
$ heroku pg:psql --app your-app-name
CREATE EXTENSION postgis;
```

In order to confirm that the installation was successful, you can run the SQL query to check the PostGIS version available:

```
=> SELECT postgis_version();

postgis_version
--------------------------------------------------
2.1 USE_GEOS=1 USE_PROJ=1 USE_STATS=1

(1 row)
```

Database tuning

Over time, it is very common that your database starts to generate some dead rows. This is a side effect generated by the **Multiversion Concurrency Control (MVCC)** mechanism of Postgres that tracks the changes in your database. The UPDATE and DELETE operations also contribute to generate these lines.

For example, when you DELETE lines, PostgreSQL doesn't remove them physically, instead it just marks them as useless. This process consumes less resources and time. The same happens when you UPDATE rows; internally Postgres performs an insert command by running the command for a new line with the same original data and marks the other one as useless.

Thus, from time to time, it is necessary to carry out some procedures for collecting the database garbage. The same will be discussed in the upcoming sections.

Database VACUUM

The VACUUM procedure is responsible for cleaning this set of useless lines in your database, thus ensuring increased performance.

Usually, the default setting of Heroku Postgres automates this procedure, but eventually you may need to perform this action manually.

The VACUUM command searches for useless lines in your database and removes them physically; this decreases the size of your database accordingly. VACUUM also organizes the records that were not deleted and, so it's guaranteed that there won't be any gaps between records.

Determining the bloat factor

You are able to determine whether your database needs a VACUUM by performing the table and index bloat query, which tells you in case there are any dead rows. Heroku offers a plugin called pg-extras to Heroku Toolbelt that allows this query to be performed.

First, install the plugin:

```
$ heroku plugins:install git://github.com/heroku/heroku-pg-extras.git
Installing heroku-pg-extras... done
```

Now you can run the pg:bloat command in order to get statistics about your database:

```
$ heroku pg:bloat DATABASE_URL --app your-app-name
type  | schemaname | object_name             | bloat | waste
------+------------+-------------------------+-------+-------
table | public     | invitations             | 11.5  | 210 MB
table | public     | selected_flight_options |  2.6  | 360 kB
```

As a result of this command, you have the bloat factor. If this is greater than 10, it indicates that this table may be experiencing degraded performance, and corrective action is recommended, especially indicated for tables larger than 100 MB.

Manual vacuuming

Before running VACUUM, it is important for you to understand that there are two main differences between the VACUUM command (without parameters) and VACUUM FULL.

The VACUUM command (without parameters) only removes tuples marked as useless in UPDATE or DELETE processes, so it is unnecessary to lock the database for operations. On the other hand, the VACUUM FULL command also removes the tuples marked as useless and it organizes the tables, removing empty gaps. To perform this process, it is necessary to lock the database in order to guarantee that no other action will be taken.

To run the VACUUM command, open the psql connection through the heroku pg:psql command:

```
$ heroku pg:psql --app your-app-name
=> VACUUM;
```

You should also run the VACUUM command in a specific table:

```
$ heroku pg:psql --app your-app-name
=> VACUUM invitations;
```

If you want to see information during the VACUUM process, you can add the VERBOSE parameter:

```
$ heroku pg:psql --app your-app-name
=> VACUUM VERBOSE;
```

Although you have the freedom to perform the VACUUM command on Heroku Postgres, it is rarely necessary to do it manually. All this can be done automatically if you configure your database properly, as it will be discussed in the upcoming section.

Automatic vacuuming

The automatic way is the most effective way to ensure the performance of your database. It allows you to configure each table or database so you are informed about when the autovacuum should be performed. For example:

```
$ heroku pg:psql --app your-app-name
=> ALTER TABLE invitations SET (autovacuum_vacuum_threshold = 60);
=> ALTER TABLE invitations SET
   (autovacuum_vacuum_scale_factor = 0.4);
```

The preceding setting sets the time that the `autovacuum` should run in your table. The threshold value defines the raw number of necessary dead lines and the scale factor defines the `bloat` factor to run the `autovacuum` process. The default values for these settings are 50 and 0.2 respectively.

With these two settings you get the real limit through the following formula:

```
vacuum threshold = autovacuum_vacuum_threshold +
  autovacuum_vacuum_scale_factor * number of rows
```

You can also impose these settings at the database level, through the following settings:

```
$ heroku pg:psql --app your-app-name
=> SELECT current_database();
current_database

------------------

d6ufnl4ugp8sq1

(1 row)

=> ALTER DATABASE d6ufnl4ugp8sq1 SET vacuum_cost_page_miss = 10;
=> ALTER DATABASE d6ufnl4ugp8sq1 SET vacuum_cost_limit = 200;
=> ALTER DATABASE d6ufnl4ugp8sq1 SET vacuum_cost_page_hit = 1;
=> ALTER DATABASE d6ufnl4ugp8sq1 SET vacuum_cost_page_dirty = 20;
```

You can find more details about each of these configuration variables in the documentation at `http://www.postgresql.org/docs/current/static/runtime-config-resource.html`.

Performance analysis

Heroku Postgres offers, through its dashboard, a graphical interface for analyzing the performance of your database.

It displays the queries through four criteria:

- **Most time consuming**
- **Slowest execution time**
- **Highest throughput**
- **Slowest I/O**

To view this information, visit `https://postgres.heroku.com`, select your database, and then go to the **Expensive queries** section.

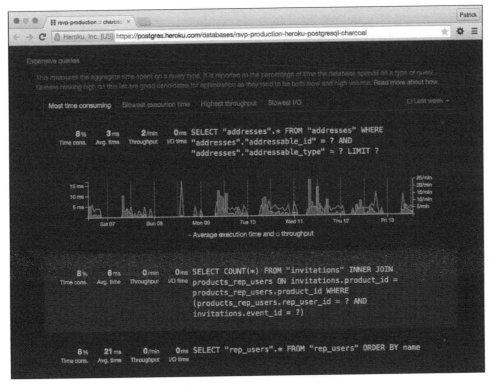

Heroku Postgres expensive queries

Self-test Questions

Answer the following questions as true or false:

1. Are the extensions functionalities that add new features in your database?

2. Is the `cube` extension used to remove accents?

3. Is the HStore extension useful to work with key value data?

4. Can you store book numbers (ISBN) in your database through the product numbering extension?

5. Does the PLV8 extension allow you to fire queries directly from inside your JavaScript code application?

6. Is the full-text extension useful for text searches across dictionaries?

7. Is it rarely possible to achieve 99% of data cache in your database on Heroku Postgres?

8. Does Heroku Postgres support PostGIS?

9. Should you always run the command VACUUM to improve the performance of your database?

10. Is Heroku Postgres able to do automatic VACUUM in your database?

Summary

In this chapter, you've learned how to use advanced features available in the Heroku Postgres platform.

These features allow you to increase the power of your database by installing extensions that add functionalities to work with data types, indexes, functions, statistics, languages, and full-text searching in your Postgres database.

You have also understood how the Heroku Postgres cache system works. It is also possible to achieve a 99.99% of data caching if your application database and application are well developed.

PostGIS was another interesting feature that you've learned in this chapter. Through this, you are able to work with geographic objects in your SQL queries. You've also noted that PostGIS is available in beta mode on Heroku Postgres.

Finally, you've understood how the tuning process works in your database. You've seen that, from time to time, useless lines are generated. In the vast majority of cases, you don't need to worry about cleaning these lines, because Heroku Postgres does it automatically for you; but, if necessary, you can perform VACUUM manually.

You have reached the end of this book and I hope your learning journey about Heroku Postgres has been very fruitful and that you have acquired all necessary knowledge to improve your work routine in this amazing platform built by Heroku. It was a great honor to help you in this learning process and I hope to see you in future books.

I say goodbye to you with a message from the great *Leonardo da Vinci*:

> *"A little knowledge puffs up; great knowledge makes humble. Blasted ears raise proud heads; those full of grain bow down."*

A
Keyword List

- **Amazon AWS EC2**: Amazon Elastic Compute Cloud (EC2) is a web service that offers resizable cloud-hosting services to make web-scale computing easier for developers. (https://aws.amazon.com/ec2/)

- **Amazon AWS S3**: Amazon Simple Storage Service (Amazon S3), provides developers and IT teams with secure, durable, and highly-scalable object storage. (https://aws.amazon.com/s3/)

- **API**: In computer programming, an application programming interface (API) is a set of routines, protocols, and tools for building software applications. (http://en.wikipedia.org/wiki/Application_programming_interface)

- **ASCII**: ASCII, abbreviated from American Standard Code for Information Interchange, is a character-encoding scheme. (http://en.wikipedia.org/wiki/ASCII)

- **Backup**: In information technology, a backup, or the process of backing up, refers to the copying and archiving of computer data so that it may be used to restore the original after a data loss event. (http://en.wikipedia.org/wiki/Backup)

- **Clojure**: This is a dynamic programming language that targets the Java Virtual Machine. (http://clojure.org/)

- **CSV**: A comma-separated values (CSV) (also sometimes called character-separated values, because the separator character does not have to be a comma) file stores tabular data (numbers and text) in plain-text form. (http://en.wikipedia.org/wiki/Comma-separated_values)

- **Data Caching**: In computing, a cache is a component that transparently stores data so that future requests for that data can be served faster. (http://en.wikipedia.org/wiki/Cache_(computing))

- **DDL**: A data definition language or data description language (DDL) is a syntax similar to a computer programming language for defining data structures, especially database schemas. (http://en.wikipedia.org/wiki/Data_definition_language)

- **Debian**: This is a Linux distribution that is composed primarily of free and open-source software, most of which is under the GNU General Public License. (https://www.debian.org/index.en.html)

- **Deploy**: Software deployment involves all the activities that make a software system available for use. (http://en.wikipedia.org/wiki/Software_deployment)

- **Dyno**: It is a lightweight linux container that runs a single user-specified command. (https://devcenter.heroku.com/articles/dynos)

- **Foreman**: It is a manager for Procfile-based applications. Its aim is to abstract away the details of the Procfile format, and allow you to run your application. (https://github.com/ddollar/foreman)

- **Gemfile**: It handles the "manages an application's dependencies" part and Gemfile.lock handles the "systematically and repeatably" part. (http://bundler.io/gemfile.html)

- **Gemfile.lock**: It turns your application into a single package of both your own code and the third-party code it ran the last time you know for sure that everything worked. (http://bundler.io/gemfile.html)

- **GIS**: A geographic information system (GIS) is a computer system designed to capture, store, manipulate, analyze, manage, and present all types of spatial data. (http://en.wikipedia.org/wiki/Geographic_information_system)

- **GiST**: In computing, GiST, or Generalized Search Tree, is a data structure and API that can be used to build a variety of disk-based search trees. (http://en.wikipedia.org/wiki/GiST)

- **GIT**: It is easy to learn and has a tiny footprint with lightning-fast performance. It outclasses SCM tools such as Subversion, CVS, Perforce, and ClearCase. (http://git-scm.com/)

- **Google Drive**: It is a file storage and synchronization service offered by Google that provides user cloud storage, file sharing, and collaborative editing. (https://www.google.com/drive/)

- **Heroku Postgres**: Heroku Postgres is the SQL database service run by Heroku. (https://www.heroku.com/postgres)

- **Heroku Toolbelt**: This is the Heroku command-line tool for working with the Heroku platform on OS X, Windows, and Debian/Ubuntu. (`https://toolbelt.heroku.com/`)

- **Heroku**: Heroku is a cloud platform as a service (PaaS) supporting several programming languages. (`https://www.heroku.com/`)

- **Hibernate**: Hibernate is an open source Java persistence framework project. Performs powerful object-relational mapping and queries databases using HQL and SQL. (`http://hibernate.org/`)

- **High Availability**: High availability is system-design approach and associated service implementation that ensures a prearranged level of operational performance will be met during a contractual measurement period. (`http://en.wikipedia.org/wiki/High_availability`)

- **HTTP**: The Hypertext Transfer Protocol (HTTP) is an application protocol for distributed, collaborative, and hypermedia information systems. (`http://en.wikipedia.org/wiki/Hypertext_Transfer_Protocol`)

- **iFrame**: The HTML iframe Element (or HTML inline frame element) represents a nested browsing context, effectively embedding another HTML page. (`http://en.wikipedia.org/wiki/IFrame`)

- **IO**: In computing, input/output or I/O (or informally, io or IO) is communication between an information processing system (such as a computer) and the outside world, possibly a human or another information processing system. (`http://en.wikipedia.org/wiki/Input/output`)

- **Java**: This is a functional computer programming language that is concurrent, class-based, object-oriented, and specifically designed to have as few implementations as possible. (`http://en.wikipedia.org/wiki/Java_(programming_language)`)

- **JavaScript**: This is a dynamic computer programming language. It is most commonly used as part of web browsers, whose implementations allow client-side scripts to interact with the user, control the browser, communicate asynchronously, and alter the document content that is displayed. (`http://en.wikipedia.org/wiki/JavaScript`)

- **JDBC**: This is a Java database connectivity technology (Java Standard Edition platform) from Oracle Corporation. (`http://en.wikipedia.org/wiki/Java_Database_Connectivity`)

- **JPA**: The Java Persistence API (JPA) is a Java programming language application programming interface specification that describes the management of relational data in applications using the Java Platform, Standard Edition and Java Platform, and Enterprise Edition. (`http://en.wikipedia.org/wiki/Java_Persistence_API`)

- **JSON**: JSON (JavaScript Object Notation) is a lightweight data-interchange format. It is easy for humans to read and write. (http://en.wikipedia.org/wiki/JSON)

- **Kernel**: In computing, the kernel is a computer program that manages input/output requests from software, and translates them into data processing instructions for the Central Processing Unit and other electronic components of a computer. (http://en.wikipedia.org/wiki/Kernel_(operating_system))

- **Logplex**: This collates log entries from all the running dynos of your app, and other components of the Heroku platform. (https://devcenter.heroku.com/articles/logplex)

- **Mac OS X**: Often called simply OS X, it is the operating system that resides on Apple's desktop and portable computer lineup. (http://en.wikipedia.org/wiki/OS_X)

- **Multitenant**: Multitenancy refers to a principle in software architecture where a single instance of the software runs on a server, serving multiple tenants. (http://en.wikipedia.org/wiki/Multitenancy)

- **Node.js**: Node.js® is a platform built on Chrome's JavaScript runtime for easily building fast, scalable network applications. (http://nodejs.org/)

- **Perl**: Perl 5 is a highly capable, feature-rich programming language with over 27 years of development. (https://www.perl.org/)

- **PGBackups**: The Heroku PGBackups add-on lets you easily capture and manage backups for your Heroku Postgres databases. (https://devcenter.heroku.com/articles/pgbackups)

- **pg_dump**: This is a utility for backing up a PostgreSQL database. (http://www.postgresql.org/docs/9.4/static/app-pgdump.html)

- **pg_restore**: This is a utility for restoring a PostgreSQL database from an archive created by pg_dump in one of the non-plain-text formats. (http://www.postgresql.org/docs/9.2/static/app-pgrestore.html)

- **pgAdmin**: This the most popular and feature-rich Open Source administration and development platform for PostgreSQL, the most advanced Open Source database in the world. (http://www.pgadmin.org/)

- **PIOPs**: This stands for Programmable Input Output System. (http://en.wikipedia.org/wiki/Programmed_input/output)

- **PLV8**: This is a shared library that provides a PostgreSQL procedural language powered by the V8 JavaScript Engine. (https://code.google.com/p/plv8js/wiki/PLV8)

- **PostGIS**: This provides spatial objects for the PostgreSQL database, allowing the storage and query of information about location and mapping. (`http://postgis.net/`)

- **Postgres.app**: This is the easiest way to get started with PostgreSQL on the Mac. (`http://postgresapp.com/`)

- **PostgreSQL**: Often simply Postgres, this is an object-relational database management system (ORDBMS). (`http://www.postgresql.org/`)

- **Procfile**: A Procfile is a list of process types in an app. (`https://devcenter.heroku.com/articles/procfile`)

- **PSQL**: The primary frontend for PostgreSQL is the psql command-line program, which can be used to enter SQL queries directly, or execute them from a file. (`http://www.postgresql.org/docs/9.4/static/app-psql.html`)

- **Python**: This is a widely used general-purpose, high-level programming language. (`https://www.python.org/`)

- **RAM**: Random-access memory (RAM) is a form of computer data storage. (`http://en.wikipedia.org/wiki/Random-access_memory`)

- **Rollback**: In database technologies, a rollback is an operation that returns the database to some previous state. (`http://en.wikipedia.org/wiki/Rollback_%28data_management%29`)

- **Ruby**: This is a programming language from Japan (available at ruby-lang.org) that is revolutionizing the Web. (`https://www.ruby-lang.org/en/`)

- **Scala**: This is an object-functional programming language for general software applications. (`http://www.scala-lang.org/`)

- **SMS**: Short Message Service (SMS) is a text messaging service component of phone, Web, or mobile communication systems. (`http://en.wikipedia.org/wiki/Short_Message_Service`)

- **Spring**: The Spring Framework provides a comprehensive programming and configuration model for modern Java-based enterprise applications. (`http://projects.spring.io/spring-framework/`)

- **SQL**: This is a special-purpose programming language designed for managing data held in a relational database management system (RDBMS), or for stream processing in a relational data stream management system (RDSMS). (`http://en.wikipedia.org/wiki/SQL`)

- **SSH**: This is a cryptographic network protocol for secure data communication, remote command-line login, remote command execution, and others. (`http://en.wikipedia.org/wiki/Secure_Shell`)

- **SSL**: This is a protocol for transmitting private documents via the Internet. (`http://www.webopedia.com/TERM/S/SSL.html`)

- **Tuning**: Database tuning describes a group of activities used to optimize and homogenize the performance of a database. (`http://en.wikipedia.org/wiki/Database_tuning`)

- **Ubuntu**: This is an open source software platform that runs everywhere from the smartphone, the tablet, and the PC to the server and the cloud. (`http://www.ubuntu.com/`)

- **URL**: A uniform resource locator (abbreviated URL; also known as a web address, particularly when used with HTTP) is a specific character string that constitutes a reference to a resource. (`http://en.wikipedia.org/wiki/Uniform_resource_locator`)

- **UUID**: A universally unique identifier (UUID) is an identifier standard used in software construction. (`http://en.wikipedia.org/wiki/Universally_unique_identifier`)

- **vCPU**: A virtual CPU (vCPU) also known as a virtual processor, is a physical central processing unit (CPU) that is assigned to a virtual machine (VM). (`http://whatis.techtarget.com/definition/virtual-CPU-vCPU`)

- **Windows**: Microsoft Windows or Windows is a metafamily of graphical operating systems developed, marketed, and sold by Microsoft. (`http://en.wikipedia.org/wiki/Microsoft_Windows`)

- **Worker**: Worker dynos can be of any process type declared in your Procfile, other than "web". Worker dynos are typically used for background jobs, queuing systems, and timed jobs. (`https://devcenter.heroku.com/articles/background-jobs-queueing`)

- **XLS**: Microsoft Excel up until the 2007 version used a proprietary binary file format called Excel Binary File Format (`.XLS`) as its primary format. (`http://en.wikipedia.org/wiki/Microsoft_Excel#File_formats`)

B
Self-test Answers

Chapter 1: Getting Started with Heroku Postgres

1. Is Heroku a multilanguage platform?

   Answer: TRUE

2. Using Heroku, does a developer have many concerns about infrastructure?

   Answer: FALSE

3. Is Heroku Toolbelt the most powerful way to manage your apps on Heroku?

   Answer: TRUE

4. Is it possible to deploy applications on Heroku via FTP?

   Answer: FALSE

5. Is dyno a virtualization of a Unix container?

   Answer: TRUE

6. Does Heroku always support the latest 10 versions of PostgreSQL?

   Answer: FALSE

7. Do the plans of the Premium tier tolerate 30 minutes of downtime?

   Answer: FALSE

8. Do all plans of Heroku run a 64-bit architecture?

   Answer: TRUE

9. Do only Standard plans have the capability of High Availability?

   Answer: FALSE

10. When a new database is built upon failure access, are the credentials changed?

    Answer: TRUE

Chapter 2: Heroku Toolbelt

1. When installing Heroku Toolbelt Standalone, is Git also provided?

   Answer: FALSE

2. Does Heroku also support web frameworks of languages such as Ruby, Java, Python, Clojure, Scala, and Node.js?

   Answer: TRUE

3. Is Foreman a tool provided to run applications locally?

   Answer: TRUE

4. To deploy a Heroku app, do we require only the source code and the dependencies file?

   Answer: FALSE

5. Does Heroku provide a web address to see apps?

   Answer: TRUE

Chapter 3: Postgres Add-on

1. Does Heroku allow duplicate application names?

   Answer: FALSE

2. Is it possible to create an application via Heroku Client and Heroku dashboard?

   Answer: TRUE

3. Is the Heroku Postgres add-on available to install in the add-ons page gallery?

   Answer: TRUE

4. When the Heroku Postgres add-on is installed, is it necessary to manually create the first database?

   Answer: FALSE

5. Does the **DATABASE_URL** variable contain information regarding the database connection?

   Answer: TRUE

6. Does the Heroku Client provide commands to work with PostgreSQL?

   Answer: FALSE

7. Is it possible to copy the Heroku database through the heroku `pg:pull` command?

   Answer: TRUE

8. Is the `heroku pg:promote` command helpful to define the main database?

   Answer: TRUE

9. Does the Heroku Postgres add-on allow connection with programming languages such as Java, Ruby, Python and Node.js?

   Answer: FALSE

10. Does Heroku Postgres allow multiple schemas in the database?

    Answer: TRUE

Chapter 4: PG Backups

1. Is it only possible to do automated backups on Heroku via add-on PG Backups?

   Answer: TRUE

2. Are the backups done by default on the primary database, available on the **DATABASE_URL** configuration variable?

   Answer: TRUE

3. Are all PG backup plans paid?

   Answer: FALSE

4. Can you download a backup via the web interface?

   Answer: TRUE

5. Are you only able to delete backups via the client?
    Answer: FALSE

6. Is the `heroku pgbackups:restore` command used to restore backups?
    Answer: TRUE

7. Is the `heroku pgbackups:url` command used to change the URL connection to the database?
    Answer: FALSE

8. Isn't it possible to restore a Heroku Postgres database locally?
    Answer: FALSE

9. Can you remove the PG Backups add-on at any time?
    Answer: TRUE

10. When the add-on Heroku Postgres is removed, are the backups kept?
    Answer: FALSE

Chapter 5: Dataclips

1. Are dataclips queries of Postgres database on Heroku can be shared?
    Answer: TRUE

2. Can dataclips be displayed in the browser?
    Answer: FALSE

3. Is it possible to download a dataclip in XLS format?
    Answer: TRUE

4. To create a dataclip, is it necessary to access the address `https://dataclips.heroku.com`?
    Answer: TRUE

5. Are dataclips not recommended for API prototyping?
    Answer: FALSE

6. Can you see the results in JSON format when adding .json in the dataclip URL?
    Answer: TRUE

7. Are dataclips shared on Google Drive never updated?

   Answer: FALSE

8. Can dataclips return an infinite set of lines?

   Answer: FALSE

9. Can you switch a dataclip to another Postgres database at any time?

   Answer: TRUE

10. Is Fork the preferred feature when you want to make a copy of a dataclip?

    Answer: TRUE

Chapter 6: Rollback, Followers, and Forks

1. Is rollback a feature that allows you to create a database in the previous state of time?

   Answer: TRUE

2. Is the `--by` flag mandatory to create a rollback database?

   Answer: FALSE

3. After creating a rollback database, is it necessary to promote a main database to activate it in your application?

   Answer: TRUE

4. Is followers an important resource for the horizontal growth of your database as master and slave?

   Answer: TRUE

5. Is the follower database synchronized automatically?

   Answer: TRUE

6. Can followers be created with different database plans?

   Answer: TRUE

7. Are forks an interesting resource for experimenting with a copy of the main database?

   Answer: TRUE

8. Does forks allow you to create a new followers and forks database with your content?

   Answer: TRUE

9. Is forks a database that is constantly synchronized with the main database?

   Answer: FALSE

10. Is the `heroku pg:wait` command useful in monitoring the new database's creation?

    Answer: TRUE

Chapter 7: Understanding Log Statements and Common Errors

1. Are logs an important information source for identifying problems in your database?

   Answer: TRUE

2. Does the heroku logs command only show database logs?

   Answer: FALSE

3. Is the postgres process necessary to filter the database logs?

   Answer: TRUE

4. Is Logplex a feature that allows a unified view of logs?

   Answer: TRUE

5. Can errors be divided in three common categories: LOG, FATAL, and PGError?

   Answer: TRUE

6. Is there an error that informs users if the query is taking more than 2 seconds?

   Answer: TRUE

7. Does the plan in the Hobby tier offer many limitations?

   Answer: TRUE

8. Should you always be careful about processes that use the same connection with the database?

   Answer: TRUE

9. Can you view important information about database metrics through the `heroku logs` command using the `heroku-postgres` filter?

    Answer: TRUE

10. Is the metrics data log with **sample#** information just examples?

    Answer: FALSE

Chapter 8: Extensions, PostGIS, Full Text Search Dictionaries, Data Caching, and Tuning

1. Are extensions functionalities that add new features in your database?

    Answer: TRUE

2. Is the extension **cube** used to remove accents?

    Answer: FALSE

3. Is the extension **HStore** useful to work with key value data?

    Answer: TRUE

4. Can you store book numbers (ISBN) in your database through the product numbering extension?

    Answer: TRUE

5. Does the **PLV8** extension allow you to fire queries directly from inside your JavaScript code application?

    Answer: FALSE

6. Is the full-text extension useful for text searches across dictionaries?

    Answer: TRUE

7. Is it rarely possible to achieve 99 percent of data cached in your database on **Heroku Postgres**?

    Answer: FALSE

8. Does Heroku Postgres support PostGIS?

    Answer: FALSE

9. Should you always run the **VACUUM** command to improve the performance of your database?

    Answer: FALSE

10. Is **Heroku Postgres** able to do automatic VACUUM in your database?

    Answer: TRUE

Index

Thank you for buying
Learning Heroku Postgres

About Packt Publishing

Packt, pronounced 'packed', published its first book, *Mastering phpMyAdmin for Effective MySQL Management*, in April 2004, and subsequently continued to specialize in publishing highly focused books on specific technologies and solutions.

Our books and publications share the experiences of your fellow IT professionals in adapting and customizing today's systems, applications, and frameworks. Our solution-based books give you the knowledge and power to customize the software and technologies you're using to get the job done. Packt books are more specific and less general than the IT books you have seen in the past. Our unique business model allows us to bring you more focused information, giving you more of what you need to know, and less of what you don't.

Packt is a modern yet unique publishing company that focuses on producing quality, cutting-edge books for communities of developers, administrators, and newbies alike. For more information, please visit our website at www.packtpub.com.

About Packt Enterprise

In 2010, Packt launched two new brands, Packt Enterprise and Packt Open Source, in order to continue its focus on specialization. This book is part of the Packt Enterprise brand, home to books published on enterprise software – software created by major vendors, including (but not limited to) IBM, Microsoft, and Oracle, often for use in other corporations. Its titles will offer information relevant to a range of users of this software, including administrators, developers, architects, and end users.

Writing for Packt

We welcome all inquiries from people who are interested in authoring. Book proposals should be sent to author@packtpub.com. If your book idea is still at an early stage and you would like to discuss it first before writing a formal book proposal, then please contact us; one of our commissioning editors will get in touch with you.

We're not just looking for published authors; if you have strong technical skills but no writing experience, our experienced editors can help you develop a writing career, or simply get some additional reward for your expertise.

Heroku Cookbook

ISBN: 978-1-78217-794-4   Paperback: 232 pages

Over 70 step-by-step recipes to solve the challenges of administering and scaling a real-world production web application on Heroku

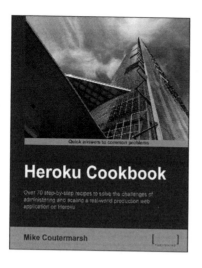

1. Make use of popular open-source projects that you'll learn to deploy and administer step-by-step.

2. Learn to effectively scale web applications while maintaining peak performance and reducing costs.

3. Get work done fast; packed with straight and to the point solutions to real-world problems that every Heroku user faces.

Heroku Cloud Application Development

ISBN: 978-1-78355-097-5   Paperback: 336 pages

A comprehensive guide to help you build, deploy, and troubleshoot cloud applications seamlessly using Heroku

1. Understand the concepts of the Heroku platform: how it works, the application development stack, and security features.

2. Learn how to build, deploy, and troubleshoot a cloud application in the most popular programming languages easily and quickly using Heroku.

3. Leverage the book's practical examples to build your own "real" Heroku cloud applications in no time.

Please check **www.PacktPub.com** for information on our titles

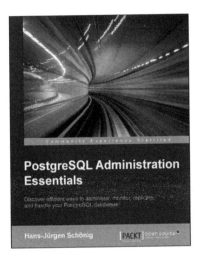

PostgreSQL Administration Essentials

ISBN: 978-1-78398-898-3   Paperback: 142 pages

Discover efficient ways to administer, monitor, replicate, and handle your PostgreSQL databases

1. Learn how to detect bottlenecks and make sure your database systems offer superior performance to your end users.

2. Replicate your databases to achieve full redundancy and create backups quickly and easily.

3. Optimize PostgreSQL configuration parameters and turn your database server into a high-performance machine capable of fulfilling your needs.

Deploying AngularJS [Video]

ISBN: 978-1-78355-447-8   Duration: 01:37 Hours

Application development and deployment made easy with AngularJS and Heroku

1. Create an easy-to-understand and flexible build system for your application using GulpJS.

2. Deploy to Heroku and add monitoring tools for error tracking.

3. Beginner-friendly introduction to writing tests and utilizing best practices.

Please check **www.PacktPub.com** for information on our titles

Made in the USA
San Bernardino, CA
27 June 2017